GRILL IT
The Italian Way

Taste Something Unusual and Make your Neighbors Drool
with these Mouthwatering Mediterranean BBQ Recipes

Alex Amalfi - Karing Ship

© Copyright: Karing Ship & Alex Amalfi 2022 - All Rights Reserved

The contents of this book may not be reproduced, duplicated, or transmitted without the direct written permission of the authors or publisher.

This book is copyrighted and intended for personal use only. You may not modify, distribute, sell, or otherwise use individual parts or the entire contents of this book without the consent of the author or publisher. Only short quotations for the purpose of reviews and/or citations on blogs and websites are allowed, with the requirement to indicate the source. Free use is allowed only for Public Domain and Creative Commons images (under the terms of the respective licenses indicated in the end notes).

Disclaimer

Please note that the information contained in this document is for informational and entertainment purposes only. Every effort has been made to present accurate, reliable and complete information. No warranty of any kind is stated or implied. By reading this document, the reader agrees that in no event shall the authors and publisher be liable for any damages or losses, direct or indirect, incurred as a result of the use of the information contained in the book, including but not limited to, - errors, omissions, or inaccuracies and to what is indicated on external sites whose links are cited. In particular, it is the sole responsibility of readers to verify that they have no allergies and/or intolerance to any of the ingredients mentioned in this book. To drink alcohol, you must be of legal drinking age in your country of residence. Drink responsibly. By continuing to read you accept all of the above conditions.

TABLE OF CONTENTS

INTRODUCTION 5
TYPICAL ITALIAN & MEDITERRANEAN SPICES, CONDIMENTS AND INGREDIENTS..9
PASTA & CO...17
    Pumpkin Tortelli 18
    Spaghetti With Seafood 20
    Rice With Sausage and Lambrusco Wine 22
    Italian Style Sandwiches 23
    Bucatini all'Amatriciana 24
    Pasta alla Genovese 25
    Strozzapreti Land and Sea 26
VEGETABLES RECIPES 29
    Various Grilled Vegetables 30
    Mediterranean Vegetable Skewers 31
    Grilled Asparagus 32
    Caramelized Celery 33
    Grilled Cauliflower 34
    Artichokes In Embers 35
    Encrusted Artichokes 36
CHEESE BASED RECIPES.. 39
    Scamorza Witha Sausage 40
    Cheese On Plates 41
    Croutons With Speck, Red Radicchio And Italian Mozzarella 42
    Grilled Pecorino Cheese 43
FISH & SEAFOOD RECIPES..45
    Glazed Tuna With Citrus Fruits 46
    Fish Fillets With Herbs 47
    Shrimps' Skewers 48
    Grilled King Prawns 49
    Octopus Salentina Style 50
    Stuffed Squids 51
    Sea & Mountain Prawns 52
    Sardines With Mediterranean Herbs 53
    Mediterranean Fish (Whole) 54
    Honey Marinated Shrimps 56

- Eel Or Capitone (Female Eel) 57
- Tuna Meatballs On Cedar Plate 58
- Scallops Land 'n Sea 59
- Sliced Fish 60
- BBQ Mussels 61
- Mackerel With Mediterranean Salad 62
- Mediterranean Fish Baked In Foil 63
- Astice* Or Lobster On Basil 64

MEAT RECIPES 67
- Lamb's Ribs 68
- Lamb's Leg 69
- Tuscan Rotisserie (Rosticciana) 70
- Pork Loin (Arista) With Mediterranean Herbs 71
- Cheeseburger With Fontina Valdostana Cheese & Tropea Onions 73
- Bologna's Mortadella 74
- Arrosticini (Sheep Skewers) 75
- A Variant Of Arrosticini 76
- The Florentine Steak 77
- The Rabbit 78
- The Boar 79
- Larded Pheasant 80
- Hare With Vegetables 81
- Apulian Lamb's Livers 82
- The Bombette (Small Bombs) 83
- The Pugliese Sausage (Cervellata) 84
- Italian Sausages 85
- Grilled Pajata 86

ABOUT THE AUTHORS 89
OTHER BOOKS FROM THE PUBLISHER 90

INTRODUCTION

A book of Italian Grill recipes, proposed in the "homeland" of this type of cooking?

What is this... a joke? Are you kidding me?

Don't you know that, in the United States, BBQ is a sacred thing? There are people who have written entire encyclopedias on the subject! Hundreds of huge cookbooks and thousands of variations on the theme, satisfy the food tastes of millions of Americans every day and here you are... with your Italian recipes?

Why not?

And I say this with the utmost respect, without the absurd pretension of teaching anything to those who are masters of this type of cuisine.

I simply think that, because Grilling is so loved in the States, there are never enough recipes and variations! And so, maybe for the lack of specific ingredients, or perhaps for simple habit, some types of "dishes" are less common there, but deserve to be tasted and appreciated on the other side of the Atlantic too.

Surely this is a cookbook dedicated to curious people, to those who are not satisfied with routine, but always want to experiment new recipes, and discover new flavors and new pleasures when they cook and when they eat.

Not to mention the possibility of making a good impression and surprising their neighbors and guests with something unusual, but always tasty and varied.

Italian Cooking, as it is known, is very tied to its territory and its ingredients, but in the modern world, so globalized and interconnected, it is no longer impossible to find and taste food from far away countries. There is almost no place where there is not some specialized Store or some Internet site that ships any product anywhere.

So, just as I here in Italy can make American-style grilled food (prepared with exactly the same products and methods) why shouldn't the opposite be possible? And as I, if I want to prepare them, rightly rely on US cookbooks... I think that, whoever wants to cook Italian, prefers to do it following the recipes of those who were born in Italy, live there and cook there every day.

The recipes I am going to propose in this book can be made (depending on the type) both with basic ingredients of Italian or Mediterranean origin only - fresh where available, or frozen - and also with equivalents easily available to US consumers. For example, local shrimps instead of Mediterranean ones.

It is FUNDAMENTAL that the Spices and Seasonings are exactly those indicated in each recipe. In fact these are the elements that characterize exclusively the Mediterranean cuisine in general and the Italian one in particular. If the original fresh ones are not available, possible alternatives are indicated. Many aromatic herbs can also be easily cultivated in pots by yourself, in order to have them always fresh at disposal.
Do not mix the seasonings (even if they are excellent) you usually use with the ones indicated in the recipes: i.e. if indicated "Lemon"... let it be a lemon, even if not Italian, maybe from California and not... Maple Syrup. If and when you want to grill Italian style... do it properly, otherwise you will have no idea what the real flavors are and you will miss how tasty all the preparations I'm suggesting are.

I repeat once again, to avoid misunderstandings: this cookbook has NO pretension to replace the real cornerstones of the American BBQ, but only to provide some more ideas or possible flavors to complement what is your usual "arsenal" of BBQ Wizards.

TYPICAL ITALIAN & MEDITERRANEAN SPICES, CONDIMENTS AND INGREDIENTS

Here is a list of the main products which characterize the Italian Typical Cuisine and of some particular ingredients which are in some cases protected by Trademark and/or Certified, in various measure, by the Italian Laws and by the European or International ones.

SPICES

Rosemary - *Rosmarinus Officinalis* grows wild all over the Mediterranean area, especially in coastal areas. It is probably the most used spice in all the countries of the Mediterranean area.

Thyme - Also *Thymus* is very common in the same areas of Rosemary, with many varieties. Particularly famous is the one from Marettimo, one of the Egadi Islands, west from Sicily.

Oregano - Another of the most common and used spices in the Italian cooking (especially the southern one) is *Origanum* - Even this one is very aromatic and tasty.

Basil - *Ocimum Basilicum*, basic ingredient of the famous Pesto alla Genovese, is not exclusive to the Mediterranean Cuisine (although it is widely used) but it is also present in many Asian cuisines.

Sage - This spice, *Salvia Officinalis*, belongs to the same family of Thyme and Mint, it grows (in its different variants) in many parts of the world.

Spearmint - *Clinopodium Nepeta*, grows mainly in mountainous areas and woods. Sometimes it is confused with Roman Mint (Mentha Pulegium) also used in Italian Cooking.

Parsley - *Petroselinum Crispum* is another of the spices very common and used in Italy, so much that it has given origin to a saying about those who are rather intrusive: "You are always around like Parsley".

Marjoram - Similar to Oregano, but more intense, *Origanum Majorana* is mainly from Italy and Greece.

Myrtle - Very common in the Mediterranean area, especially in Sardinia, *Myrtus Communis*, is used both as a spice and as the base of the famous liqueur which takes its name and is consumed as a digestive at the end of meals.

Juniper - *Juniperus Communis* is spread in the whole Northern Hemisphere, used in many cuisines and it is the base of Gin liqueur.

Hot Pepper - The numerous variants of the genus *Capsicum* are spread all over the world. In Italy is particularly appreciated the Calabrian hot pepper, however there are many others.

Capers - Widespread in the whole Mediterranean area, as well as in Western Asia, *Capparis Spinosa* are indispensable elements in some of the dishes proposed in this cookbook. They can be preserved in oil, vinegar and salt. The latter are absolutely to be preferred. Before using them, they must be desalinated in a cup with cold water and then gently rinsed under running water. Particularly appreciated by gourmets are those produced in the island of Pantelleria.

CONDIMENTS

Extra Virgin Olive Oil (EVO)

When we talk about Extra Virgin Olive Oil (EVO) we are talking about the fundamental and characterizing pillar of the so called Mediterranean Diet in general and of Italian Cooking in particular. The oil extracted from olives has, in fact, over the centuries, characterized the main difference between the condiments used in continental countries, compared to those along the Mediterranean coast. The plant, in fact, grows only at particular latitudes and up to low hill altitudes.
What is it that characterizes EVO Oil as opposed to other condiments of animal origin such as butter? Basically it is the presence of Unsaturated Fatty Acids which, as it has been proved, have beneficial effects on fat metabolism, as opposed to animal fats. It can be used both raw, to dress salads and other foods, in normal cooking and, above all, in fried foods, thanks to its higher "Smoke Point" which allows it to withstand very well the temperatures required for frying.
To be defined as EXTRA-VIRGIN OLIVE OIL, an oil must have an acidity value of less than 0.8% and must be obtained by COLD EXTRACTION using MECHANICAL METHODS.
EVO Oil must be stored with care, away from light (hence the dark and opaque bottles) and from heat sources. Moreover, it is not recommended to use it after one year from production, as it loses most of its properties and characteristics.

Unfortunately, this is a product which is often subject to frauds and adulteration. We therefore particularly recommend to carefully check the origin of the oil which, first of all, must be produced in Italy, from Italian olives and certified with the D.O.P. mark (Denominazione di Origine Protetta). Be wary of cheap oils, because the minimum production costs are rather high and therefore it may not be an oil of Italian origin and with the physical-chemical-organoleptic characteristics of EVO.

Most of the Italian EVO is produced in Apulia (more than 75%) decreasing as one goes north. The most famous is the EVO of Bitonto (Ba). Excellent EVO oils are found particularly in Lazio, Umbria and Tuscany.

In order to be used in Mediterranean Cuisine, in case you are not able to find a valid Italian EVO, an alternative can be EVO from Spain and Greece, but always make sure they have a recognized certification mark.

Balsamic Vinegar

Balsamic Vinegar originates and is produced (with different methods) EXCLUSIVELY in the provinces of Modena and Reggio Emilia. These products are identified with the certification "ACETO BALSAMICO DI MODENA" D.O.P. - "ACETO BALSAMICO DI REGGIO EMILIA" D.O.P. and "ACETO BALSAMICO DI MODENA " I.G.P. (Indicazione Geografica Protetta). Be wary of any other imitation or denomination.

As with EVO oil, these marks and the references required by law must be present in ITALIAN on the product label.

Why is it important for products to be certified? Because the production regulations established by law, not only certify the origin, but also the types of processing from which depend the chemical-physical and organoleptic characteristics.

What characterizes the typical cuisines of every country in the world (and especially Italy) are the traditions, the origin, the cultivation and the treatments of specific products. In order to best appreciate (and safely) traditional recipes it is therefore essential to use original and certified products.

INGREDIENTS

(we mention only the most important and common ones)

Parmiggiano Reggiano

With a centuries-old tradition, this famous (and delicious) hard paste cow cheese is protected by the D.O.P. mark and it is produced EXCLUSIVELY in the provinces of Modena, Reggio Emilia, Parma and Bologna, according to a strict production disciplinary. It is available in different lengths of seasoning. The longer the length, the greater the value.

WARNING: Parmesan Cheese has nothing to do with Original Parmiggiano Reggiano and is an attempt to make consumers outside the European Union believe they are using the original. Obviously the flavor and nutritional qualities are NOT even close to those of D.O.P. Parmiggiano Reggiano.

Grana Padano

Also this cheese (similar, but not equal to Parmiggiano Reggiano) has a long tradition and is protected in the European Union by the D.O.P. mark.
Production is located in Piedmont, Lombardy, Trentino-Alto Adige and Emilia Romagna.

Mortadella di Bologna

A Classic of Italian charcuterie. There are many varieties, but the ideal one is the one bearing the I.G.P. mark.

Cipolla Rossa di Tropea

This vegetable is a particular type of onion (Allium Cepa) cultivated exclusively in some areas of Calabria. It is protected by the mark I.G.P. (Protected Geographical Indication). Its organoleptic characteristics have made it famous throughout the world and there is hardly a chef who has not tried his hand at a recipe using it.

Cipolla Rossa di Acquaviva delle Fonti

It has a flatter shape and a lighter color than the previous one, it also has a more delicate taste. Its production is very limited, in the area of Acquaviva delle Fonti, in the province of Bari and for this reason, it is less known and spread.
Also in this case, it is protected by a Trademark: the D.O.P. one.

NOTE: It is important that, in case a recipe of this book mentions any of the condiments or ingredients just listed, it is strongly recommended to use (as far as possible) the original ones, protected by their respective trademarks. The use of alternative foods will in fact compromise the success and the final quality of the dish you will prepare.

In case of spices, we always suggest the use of products (dried or frozen) coming from Italy, as indicated in the single recipes. In case the use of fresh products is foreseen, the ideal would be that you grow them yourself, starting from seeds or plants of Italian origin. In most cases it is very easy and they even grow in small pots. Otherwise, buy them fresh locally.

PINZIMONIO: A TYPICAL SIDE DISH

Pinzimonio is a typical Italian side dish well known since the Renaissance and it is widely used during summer grills, to accompany both meat and fish. It is a very simple side dish, made of Extra Virgin Olive Oil (EVO), Salt, Ground Pepper and eventually, a dash of Wine Vinegar, in which are dipped some raw vegetables, also typical of the Italian countryside.
Of course, vegetables must be fresh and well cleaned.
The most used ones (also because it is easier to eat them with hands) are:
Celery Ribs
Carrots
Fennel
Red Radishes

More rarely:
Peppers in strips
Spring onions

WINES

As for wines suggested to accompany recipes, it is practically impossible to indicate a specific brand and its label. There are thousands and thousands of them, and it is a utopia to think they are all distributed abroad in the same way. We therefore limited to indicating the type of wine, however we recommend to choose only bottles that clearly show in the label, one of the following Marks of Protection:

D.O.C.G. - Denominazione di Origine Controllata e Garantita (Denomination of Controlled and Guaranteed Origin)
D.O.C. - Denominazione di Origine Controllata (Denomination of Controlled Origin)
I.G.P. - Indicazione Geografica Protetta (Protected Geographical Indication)
I.G.T. - Indicazione Geografica Tipica (Typical Geographical Indication)

The absence of these marks exposes the consumer to risks of frauds and adulterations. Not to mention the poor quality of the wine itself.

PASTA & CO.

Pumpkin Tortelli

GRILL IT — The Italian Way

Description:

What could be more Italian than Pasta? Pasta is in fact our National Dish par excellence and, in the collective imagination, Italy and Pasta are considered almost synonymous. Both in a positive sense, and even in a negative one. The derogatory term "mangiaspaghetti" is a classic example.
Back to Cooking... cooking Pasta on the Grill, even though it is not at all usual, has its own reason for being for some particular recipes, such as this one I am presenting to you, which also includes homemade Pasta.

Preparation: Long - Cooking: Medium

What's needed . 4 people

- Hard Wheat Flour – 0.77 lb.
- Fresh Eggs - 3
- Milk – 8.45 oz.
- Parmiggiano Reggiano – 0.26 lb. (alternatively, Grana Padano)
- Seasoned Italian Pecorino Cheese – 0.44 lb.
- Pumpkin (pulp) 0.88 lb.
- Shelled Walnuts - 3 or 4 (Optional)
- Extra Virgin Olive Oil
- Water
- Salt
- Ground Black Pepper

How to Prepare

First of all you will need to prepare the pastry for the Tortelli.
Clean well a work surface in your kitchen and then form with the flour a truncated cone with a hollow at the top.
Inside this hollow, open the Eggs and add about 3.5 oz. of warm Water.
Knead well with your hands, until you obtain a homogeneous and smooth ball of dough on the surface.
Now roll out the dough with a rolling pin (or use a pasta machine) until it becomes a sheet about 0.06 in. thick.
Using a pastry cutter, form squares of 1.57 – 2.36 in. per side.

Cooking the Pumpkin: directly on the Grill, at a medium temperature (265 - 300 °F) for half an hour, until the flesh is soft.

Once the pumpkin is cooked, mix well the pumpkin pulp and the grated Parmiggiano Reggiano in

GRILL IT — The Italian Way

a bowl. Add a pinch of salt and ground black pepper. An excellent alternative is to add some finely ground walnut kernels to the mixture.

Now you will have to distribute this mixture in the center of the Pasta squares you prepared earlier. Use only half of the squares. Then form small balls. Then place another square of dough on top and with your fingers, press the edges well. Alternatively, you can use all the squares, with the ball in the center, then taking one corner of the dough, overlap it to the one in front and press it with your fingers. Next, take the other two corners and, giving the Tortello a circular shape, close them together.

In this video, you can see the job done in just a few seconds. (https://youtu.be/PWmJtG7O_xk)

In a separate pan, heat the milk and slowly pour in the grated Pecorino cheese. Stir well until you obtain a creamy consistency.

Now pour a drizzle of Evo Oil over the Tortelli and, using a small brush, grease their surfaces well, then distribute them on a perforated tray and place it directly on the grill. The temperature should be between 230 and 265 °F. Let them cook for 6 to 8 minutes, until they lighten.

Now you can distribute them on the plates and pour the cream with Pecorino on top.

Recommended Wines: Syrah (Sicily) or Vernaccia di San Gimignano (Tuscany)

Spaghetti With Seafood

GRILL IT — The Italian Way

Description:

Whoever has been visiting Italy has surely had the opportunity to taste some pasta dishes with seafood, often called "allo Scoglio". Mussels and clams are the masters, but also Telline, Razor Clams, Lupini Marini and others are variously used according to local availability.
Here I will propose the classic basic dish: Spaghetti with Mussels and Clams, which if cooked on the barbecue, will have a truly amazing result. Even with this dish you will certainly amaze your guests and you will be recognized as Masters of BBQ!

Preparation: Medium - Cooking: Fast

What's needed . per person

- Fresh Mussels: at least 0.35 lb. - Alternatively, you can use frozen ones (0.22 lb. - without the shells)
- Fresh Real Clams: at least 0.2 lb. - Alternatively, you can use frozen (0.11 lb. - without the shells)
- Italian Spaghetti – 0.26 lb.
- Extra Virgin Olive Oil (EVO)
- Oregano - Best if Fresh
- Basil - Best if Fresh
- Dried Italian Chili Pepper - Preferably from Calabria
- Salt

How to Prepare

If the seafood is fresh (with the shell) wash and clean it well (especially the mussels) with a small brush. Then leave them to soak in cold water for at least an hour.
If they are frozen, you can also skip this phase and cook them a few minutes after they have been taken out of the freezer.

Boil plenty of water with a handful of coarse salt, where you will then blanch the pasta for 3 or 4 minutes.
Turn on the BBQ and set it for Direct Cooking at maximum temperature (> 445 °F).

Place a large frying pan or a Wok on the grill with 2 tablespoons of EVO oil and half a clove of garlic per person. Let it brown, making sure that the oil does not smoke.

At this point, add mussels and clams with their shells after draining them and cook until the shells open.

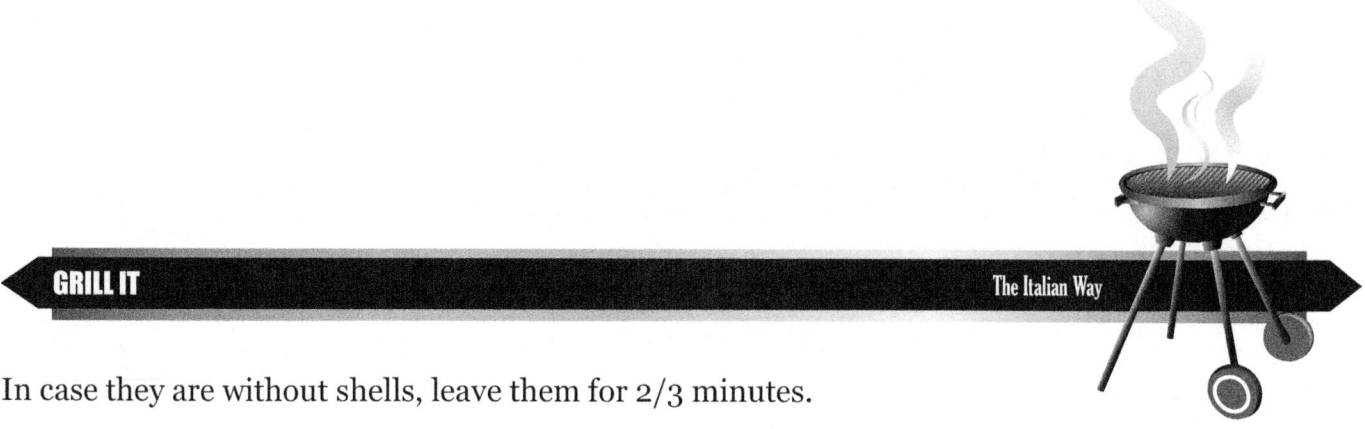

In case they are without shells, leave them for 2/3 minutes.

Now add the Pasta (drained) that you have cooked in boiling water for 3 or 4 minutes. Stir well and add a pinch of chopped oregano and ground chili pepper. Close the lid of the Barbecue or, failing that, cover the pan. Continue to cook for about 10 minutes, stirring occasionally and checking that the Spaghetti is not too soft... but not too hard either.

Bring to the table and get ready for a standing ovation!

Recommended Wines: Ribolla Gialla (Friuli Venezia Giulia) or Falanghina del Sannio (Campania)

Rice With Sausage And Lambrusco Wine

GRILL IT The Italian Way

Description:

A sumptuous first course, in the full tradition of a region (Emilia Romagna) which has given so much to the prestige of Italian cuisine, here revisited for grilling.

As we are talking about rice, I would like to remind you that for centuries rice growing has been another of Italy's pride and joy. To discover some of the best Rices currently in production, we suggest you to have a look at this LINK, where we have selected 5 of the most prestigious Italian producers. There are some absolutely unmissable "goodies" for people who like this extraordinary cereal. Don't worry: it's written in English too!

Preparation: Quick - Cooking: Quick

What's needed. 4 people

- Carnaroli Rice (alternatively, you can use the Vialone Nano variety) – 0.9 lb.
- Pure Pork Sausages – 0.77 lb.
- Lambrusco di Sorbara D.O.C. "Amabile" – 10.15 oz.
- Parmiggiano Reggiano D.O.P. - 0.30 lb.
- Butter – 0.15 lb.
- Vegetable Broth – 0.4 gal.
- Ground Black Pepper
- Salt

How to Prepare

First light your Barbecue and set it for Direct Cooking at about 360 °F.

Remove the skin from the sausages and crumble it a little. You will need to form pieces that are not too large.

Now place a grill pan on the grill and place the sausage pieces in it. After 3 or 4 minutes, add the dry Rice, so that it can toast. At this point pour in the wine and let it evaporate completely.

Pour in about 17 oz of warmed stock, add a pinch of salt and close the lid of the grill. Alternatively, cover the pan directly.

Every 2 to 3 minutes, add a ladle or two of broth. The total cooking time will be 15-20 minutes (from when you first add the broth) depending on the type of rice you used.

At the end, remove the risotto from the grill and pour the grated Parmiggiano Reggiano, butter, a pinch of ground pepper into the pan and stir well (adding more broth if necessary) until the risotto is perfectly creamy.

Now, all you have to do is serve and enjoy this delicacy.

Recommended Wines: Lambrusco di Sorbara D.O.C. Secco (Emilia-Romagna) or Bonarda dell'Oltrepò Pavese (Lombardy)

Italian Style Sandwiches

GRILL IT — The Italian Way

Description:

Well, I certainly don't have to teach you how to make great sandwiches. The ones I am proposing differ only for most of the ingredients, which are clearly of Mediterranean origin. Let's say a more or less broad "variation on the theme" of what you usually do. On the other hand, cooking is also constantly experimenting... otherwise, you get bored.

Preparation: Quick - Cooking: Quick

What's needed.

The quantities of each ingredient are up to you, depending on your appetite

- Oil sandwiches of elongated or round shape
- Red Onion of Tropea I.G.P.
- Italian Mozzarella
- Balsamic Vinegar of Modena D.O.P.
- Basil Pesto
- Extra Virgin Olive Oil (EVO)
- Calabrian Nduja of Spilinga (particular type of spicy and soft salami)
- Fresh Calabrian Chilli Pepper
- Garlic in Slices. I suggest you try the one from Sulmona if you can find it
- Fresh Pepperoni
- Salt
- Ground Pepper

How to Prepare

Cut the pepperoni into strips and the fresh peppers into small pieces.
Mix (indicative amounts for each sandwich) a tablespoon of EVO oil, 1 clove of chopped garlic, 1 teaspoon of balsamic vinegar, a piece of chopped onion, a few pieces of chopped hot pepper, salt and pepper.

Lightly heat the Panini cut in half, placing them with the crumb side down directly on the grill.

Now spread a little bit of Pesto on one half of the sandwich, then add the Mozzarella in cubes or slices, a little bit of Nduja di Spilinga (beware that it is very spicy!) a little bit of Garlic and Onion Mix and a couple of strips of Peppers. Close the sandwich and put it back on the grill, with the lid closed.

Temperature and cooking time? Why ask me? You know how to do it!

Suggested wines: Beer, only beer, nothing but beer!

Bucatini All'Amatriciana

GRILL IT — The Italian Way

Description:

Caution! Because here we are entering a "minefield". When it comes to the workhorse of Roman cuisine in particular, or of Lazio in general, one reads and hears about everything. The different interpretations (in terms of types of ingredients) that you see around are 99% exercises of fantasy that have nothing to do with Traditional Recipes. There is only one way to prepare Amatriciana, just as there is only one way to prepare Gricia and Carbonara. And there are "historical" reasons that explain all this: first of all the fact that these recipes derive from sheep farming. As a consequence, it is not that shepherds, in past centuries, could go shopping at the supermarket, but they prepared their daily meals with what little they had available and which could be easily preserved. So, if you want to be sure to cook "Roman style"... strictly follow what I am going to tell you and do not make any variations on the theme. Or at least... don't call it Amatriciana, but give it another name!

Preparation: Quick - Cooking: Quick

What's needed. 4 people

- Bucatini (alternatively you can use Italian Spaghetti) – 1 lb.
- Pork jowl (or Pork cheek) of Amatrice or Norcia (not Bacon) – 0.45 lb.
- Peeled Tomatoes (San Marzano) – 0.55 lb.
- Pecorino Romano D.O.P. - 0.26 lb.
- Coarse salt
- Ground Black Pepper

How to Prepare

Set your grill for direct cooking, at 350 °F.
In the meantime, boil a couple of liters (0.45 gal) of water in a pot. When it boils, add a handful of Coarse Salt.

Now place a Wok on the grill and add the Guanciale cut into small pieces. At this point, the fat will melt on its own and the pieces will take on a crispy appearance. Remove them by draining them in the same Wok and set them aside. Now pour into the Wok the Peeled Tomatoes cut into two or three pieces, stir well and cook, stirring occasionally for 10 - 12 minutes at least.

While the tomatoes are on the grill, cook the Bucatini (or Spagetti) in boiling water for 3 to 4 minutes. Then drain them and pour them into the Wok, letting them cook for about 10 minutes, adding a little of the Pasta Cooking Water halfway through cooking.

At the end, remove the pasta, add the Guanciale, plenty of grated Pecorino Romano D.O.P. and a sprinkling of ground pepper.

Now assume an appearance of detached and (almost) modest superiority, while your guests enjoy in amazement this marvel that you have, so magnanimously, prepared for them!

Recommended Wines: Petit Verdot (Lazio) or Cesanese del Piglio (Lazio)

Pasta Alla Genovese

GRILL IT — The Italian Way

Description:
Despite the name may sound otherwise, Sugo alla Genovese is a recipe of Neapolitan Tradition. It seems that this is due to the fact that in a now distant past, many cooks of the Partenopean Trattorias were originally from Genoa. The fact is that this dish has become a "Classic"... one of the many not to be missed when visiting Naples. A few small modifications are necessary to cook it on the barbecue, but you will not be disappointed.

Preparation: Quick - Cooking: Long

What's needed. 4 people

- Picanha (in the original recipe is used the Girello) – 1.1 lb.
- Paccheri of Gragnano – 0.88 lb.
- Extra Virgin Olive Oil (EVO)
- Onion - 2 medium
- Meat Broth
- Vinegar
- Parsley
- Salt
- Ground Black Pepper

How to Prepare

The cooking of this recipe will be done in two phases. The first one will concern the smoking of the Meat with the indirect method, while the second one will continue with the direct one.

First of all, wash, clean and cut the beef into small pieces and then place it on the grill for smoking (use the chips you prefer).

Once the smoking process is complete, prepare the embers for direct cooking at 360 - 390 °F and place a special cast iron pan (Cocotte) on the grill in which to pour the finely chopped onion and a bit of EVO oil.
When the onion is well browned, add the Picanha and the meat broth, so that it covers the meat completely. Put the lid on the pan and let it cook for a long time, until the Meat has become completely frayed.

At this point, boil the Paccheri for 7 to 8 minutes, then drain them and add them to the Meat in the Cocotte, along with a splash of Vinegar. Stir carefully for 3 to 4 minutes, so that everything is well mixed.

Now serve at the table and enjoy the success!

Recommended Wine: Taurasi (Campania) or Rosso Costa d'Amalfi Campania)

Strozzapreti Land And Sea

GRILL IT — The Italian Way

Description:

Strozzapreti (of Romagna origin) are just one example. You can in fact experiment with this recipe also with many of the countless varieties of fresh Italian pasta. The important thing is that they are of the "short" type. E.g. Orecchiette or Turcinieddi Pugliesi, Gnocchetti Sardi and so on.

Preparation: Quick - Cooking: Medium

What to Serve . per person

- Eggplants (preferably long black ones) – 0.25 lb.
- Squid (fresh) – 10.22 lb.
- Fresh Italian Pasta (short, Strozzapreti type) – 0.28 lb.
- Italian Buffalo Mozzarella – 0.18 lb.
- Extra Virgin Olive Oil (EVO)
- Garlic - 1 clove
- Fresh Basil – 0.35 ounce
- Italian White Wine – 1.8 oz.
- Ground Black Pepper
- Salt

How to Prepare

Start by washing and cleaning the Calamari, then cut them into very small pieces.
Next, wash the eggplants, peel them and then cut them into small cubes. The peels can then be placed in the embers to get a smoky aroma.
Fry the eggplant using EVO oil and put them aside on a sheet of kitchen paper, to absorb the excess of Oil.

Now set up your grill for direct cooking at a temperature of around 360 °F.
Place a large frying pan or a cast iron Wok on the grill with a drizzle of EVO oil, garlic cloves and chopped basil. After a couple of minutes, add the white wine. Then pour in the diced squid and fried eggplant. Remove the Wok from the grill and cover it with a lid.

In a pot with plenty of boiling water and a handful of coarse salt, blanch the Strozzapreti for 2 or 3 minutes, then drain them well and pour them into the Wok along with the Mozzarella (also in small cubes), a drizzle of Evo Oil, a pinch of Salt and a sprinkling of Ground Pepper.
Put the pan back on the grill (at this point, you can pour the eggplant skins directly onto the embers for a light smoke). Stir well and let it cook for another 8 - 10 minutes.

Serve and then... No comment!

Suggested Wines: Cirò Rosè (Calabria) or Maremma Toscana Rosè (Tuscany)

VEGETABLES RECIPES

Various Grilled Vegetables

GRILL IT — The Italian Way

Description:

This is another simple dish that can be prepared and cooked in just a few minutes. The Italian character in this case is given exclusively by the type of vegetables and the seasoning with Extra Virgin Olive Oil and Mediterranean Spices.

Preparation: Easy - Cooking: Quick

What's needed . 4 people

- Seasonal Fresh Vegetables*
- * Zucchini Romanesche - Small tomatoes (Pachino's cherries or datterini) - Tomatoes - Eggplants (long, black or round) - Peppers - Onions (red of Tropea or Acquaviva delle Fonti) - Leeks.
- Garlic
- Aromas - Oregano, Basil, Rosemary, Thyme (preferably fresh, but dried ones are good too) - Black Pepper
- Extra Virgin Olive Oil (EVO)
- Salt

How to Prepare

After having thoroughly cleaned the vegetables and peeled the onions, cut them lengthwise (or into rounds, depending on their shape) into fairly thin slices (about 0.4 in.). The cherry tomatoes, on the other hand, should be cut in half.

Arrange the different pieces on a well-cleaned grill at moderate heat. Cooking times vary from 3 to 7/8 minutes per side, depending on the type of vegetable and the thickness of the slices. In general, Zucchini are much faster, whereas Peppers and Eggplants require a longer cooking time. Vegetables need to be turned only once.

When they are ready, arrange the slices and rounds on a serving plate, and sprinkle with a pinch of Salt, finely chopped Garlic, Ground Black Pepper and the flavors of your choice. To finish, a drizzle of EVO oil will complete the work.

Note that grilled vegetables are much tastier if eaten after they have cooled and absorbed the seasoning.

Recommended Wines: Malvasia Puntinata (Lazio), or Falanghina (Campania).

Mediterranean Vegetable Skewers

GRILL IT — The Italian Way

Description:

An extremely simple preparation, which owes its main characteristic to some ingredients and seasonings typically Mediterranean, and especially to the Red Onions of Tropea. The latter in fact, are practically a "Unicum" appreciated all over the world. Their sweetness makes them a very characteristic element of the dishes in which they are used.

An equally valid alternative - but less known and spread - are Acquaviva delle Fonti Onions.

These skewers can be served as side dishes, or as the main course of a vegetarian barbecue. In these cases, you can also double the doses.

Preparation: Easy - Cooking: Quick

What's needed . 4 people

- Red onions of Tropea - 2
- Peppers (Yellow or Red) - 2
- Eggplants (Long and Narrow type) – 0.55 lb
- Whole Cultivated Mushrooms - 0,55 lb
- Zucchini - 0,55 lb
- Cherry or date tomatoes (Pachino tomatoes are ideal) – 0.55 lb

- Extra Virgin Olive Oil (EVO) – 5.1 oz
- Wine Vinegar – 3.4 oz.
- Balsamic Vinegar - ½ Spoonful
- Garlic - 1 or 2 Cloves (depending on size)
- Cane Sugar - 1 Teaspoon
- Salt
- Black Pepper

How to Prepare

Start by preparing the dressing, combining the EVO Oil, Wine Vinegar and Balsamic Vinegar, finely chopped Garlic, Sugar and a pinch of Salt. Mix well and add a sprinkling of Ground Black Pepper.

Next, clean each vegetable (remove only the first thin layer from the onions) and cut them into 1.2/1.5 in pieces. Dress them with a drizzle of EVO oil and keep them separated according to the type of vegetables. Then mount the pieces on steel skewers. Each vegetable should be mounted on different skewers so that you can better control the different cooking times.

Place the skewers on the grill, which is already hot over moderate heat, and cook for between 3 and 6 minutes per side.

Once the vegetables are cooked, place them on a tray and pour on the previously prepared condiment.

Recommended Wines: Orvieto Bianco Classico (Umbria) or EST EST di Montefiascone (Lazio).

Grilled Asparagus

GRILL IT — The Italian Way

Description:

A rather unusual way to cook these very popular and appreciated vegetables, but definitely appetizing. With these you will surely amaze your guests! In addition, preparation and cooking are quick and easy.

Preparation: Quick - Cooking: Quick

What's needed . 4 people

- Asparagus - 1 bunch
- Sicilian Lemon - 1 (Optional)
- Extra virgin olive oil (EVO) – 1.7 oz.
- Salt
- White pepper

How to Prepare

Clean the Asparagus and cut off the end of the stalks.
Mix the EVO Oil, a pinch of Salt and a pinch of Ground White Pepper in a bowl large enough to hold the Asparagus.
Dip the Asparagus in the liquid, turning them well to season them evenly.
Prepare the Barbecue for direct cooking, with a temperature between 360 and 410°F.
Place the Asparagus on top of a Matt Grill (if available), or crosswise on the grill.
Close the lid.
Let the asparagus cook between 4 and 7 minutes (depending on thickness), turning them a couple of times, until they are evenly browned. Be careful not to burn them!
Place them on a serving plate, season with a little more olive oil and, if necessary, a bit of lemon juice.

Recommended Wines: Grillo (Sicily) or Vernaccia di San Gimignano (Tuscany)

Caramelized Celery

GRILL IT — The Italian Way

Description:

This is just a tasty accompaniment to a good ice cream to be eaten at the end of the meal. But since you will have turned on your Barbecue and at the end there will be only the embers left not too hot... why not take advantage?

Preparation: Easy - Cooking: Quick

What's needed.

- Celery stalks
- Cane Sugar

How to Prepare

Wash the celery stalks and peel off the outside.
Boil a pot of water and add a teaspoon of brown sugar to each celery stalk.
Let the stalks soften and then, after draining them, transfer them to a clean corner of the grill. The coals will need to be warm. Turn it several times until it has taken on a caramelized appearance.

Recommended Wines: Sciacchetrà delle Cinque Terre (Liguria) or Vin Santo (Tuscany)

Grilled Cauliflower

GRILL IT — The Italian Way

Description:

Cauliflower, in its different varieties, is a very common winter vegetable used in many different types of traditional cooking. If you have a vegetable garden, we suggest you try growing a particular variety, which is much sweeter and tastier than normal: Broccolo Romanesco. In the months when it is colder it is really delicious (https://en.wikipedia.org/wiki/Romanesco_broccoli).
Doing it on the grill is not very common, but it is certainly worth a try.

Preparation: Quick - Cooking: Medium

What's needed . per person

- Cauliflower (or Romanesco Broccoli) – 0.55 lb.
- Extra Virgin Olive Oil (EVO)
- Chopped dried chilli of Calabria (Optional)
- Amalfi Coast or Sicily Lemons - 1/2
- Salt

How to Prepare

Clean and wash the cauliflower and remove the outer leaves.
Dress generously with EVO oil, a pinch of chopped chilli pepper if desired, and salt to taste.
Place the Cauliflower on a sheet of aluminum foil for cooking and screw it up to half height.

Set the BBQ for indirect cooking at a low temperature (between 210 and 250 °F) and cook the cauliflower for at least 60 minutes. The final consistency should be quite soft.

Remove it from the grill and let it cool a little bit. Then cut it into pieces and serve at the table as a side dish with some other preparation. I particularly like it at room temperature, so not too hot, perhaps further seasoned with a drizzle of raw EVO oil and the juice of ½ Lemon.

Recommended Wines: Traminer Aromatico (Trentino Alto Adige) or Malvasia Puntinata (Lazio)

Artichokes In Embers

GRILL IT　　　　　　　　　　　　　　　　　　　　　　　The Italian Way

Description:

Artichoke is a very appreciated vegetable, which is prepared in many different ways. However, it's seldom considered for grilling. The recipe that I suggest here involves cooking them straight into the embers. The result will be decidedly unusual and surprising.

Preparation: Easy - Cooking: Quick

What's needed . per person

- Artichokes - 2 (medium-large)
- Extra Virgin Olive Oil (EVO)
- Lemon - 1
- Coarse Salt
- Peppercorns

How to Prepare

Wash the artichokes well, cut off the stalks leaving only about 2 in. of them. Also remove any leaves and leave all the scales. Cut off the tip of the artichoke (about 0.8 in.) and put the prepared ones in a container with water and lemon juice. Let them rest for half an hour.

Prepare a thick layer of embers so that it takes on a whitish and homogeneous consistency (i.e., medium-low heat).

Now place the artichokes directly in the middle of the coals with the cutted tips upwards (use protective gloves).
Now wait until the outer layer is completely charred. This will take between 8 and 12 minutes.
At this point, still using the gloves, pour a drizzle of EVO Oil on the cuts (do not let it go on the embers) along with a few grains of Salt and Pepper. Here you can "experiment" with different flavors of Salt and different varieties of Pepper.

Cook for another 10 - 14 minutes. If necessary, tear off a piece of the inner leaves and taste it, to see if it is soft enough. In this case, you can consider the cooking as completed.

Serve at the table and, of course, do not eat the charred outside... but only the tender hearts inside. You will be pleasantly surprised!

Recommended Wines: Frascati Bianco (Lazio) or Nero d'Avola (Sicily)

Encrusted Artichokes

GRILL IT  The Italian Way

Description:
Here is another recipe based on Artichokes, but this time more than an accompaniment, they will be both a dish and a side dish, given the presence of sausage and pasta sheets.

Preparation: Quick - Cooking: Quick

What's needed . 4 people

- Artichokes (possibly "Romaneschi") - 2 per Person
- Sausages – 0.8 lb.
- Ready Puff Pastry - 1 Package
- Medium Eggs - 2
- Yellow Potatoes - 3 small
- Sicilian Lemons - 2
- Ground Black Pepper
- Salt

How to Prepare

Clean the artichokes carefully. Cut off the tips by about 0.5 in. and leave only 2 in. of stems. Remove all the outer scales and keep only the inner hearts. Cut them in two in the direction of the longest part.

Now leave the artichokes in a container with water and lemon juice for at least half an hour.

Then, in a pot with plenty of boiling water, blanch the Artichokes and Potatoes for a few minutes.

Mash potatoes and add the sausage pulp (remove the skin) with a pinch of salt and pepper. Mix well and, with this mixture, stuff the single pieces of Artichokes.

Now cut as many squares of puff pastry as there are pieces of Artichokes, place 1 piece in the center and cover it completely with the pastry.

Beat the eggs in an appropriate container.

The Grill must be set up for Indirect Cooking, at a temperature between 340 and 375 °F.
I recommend using a special ceramic plate to place on the grill. Place the Artichokes on the plate and brush them with beaten Eggs.

Let them cook until the puff pastry is completely golden brown.

Recommended Wines: Dolcetto (Piedmont) or Teroldego Rotaliano (Alto Adige)

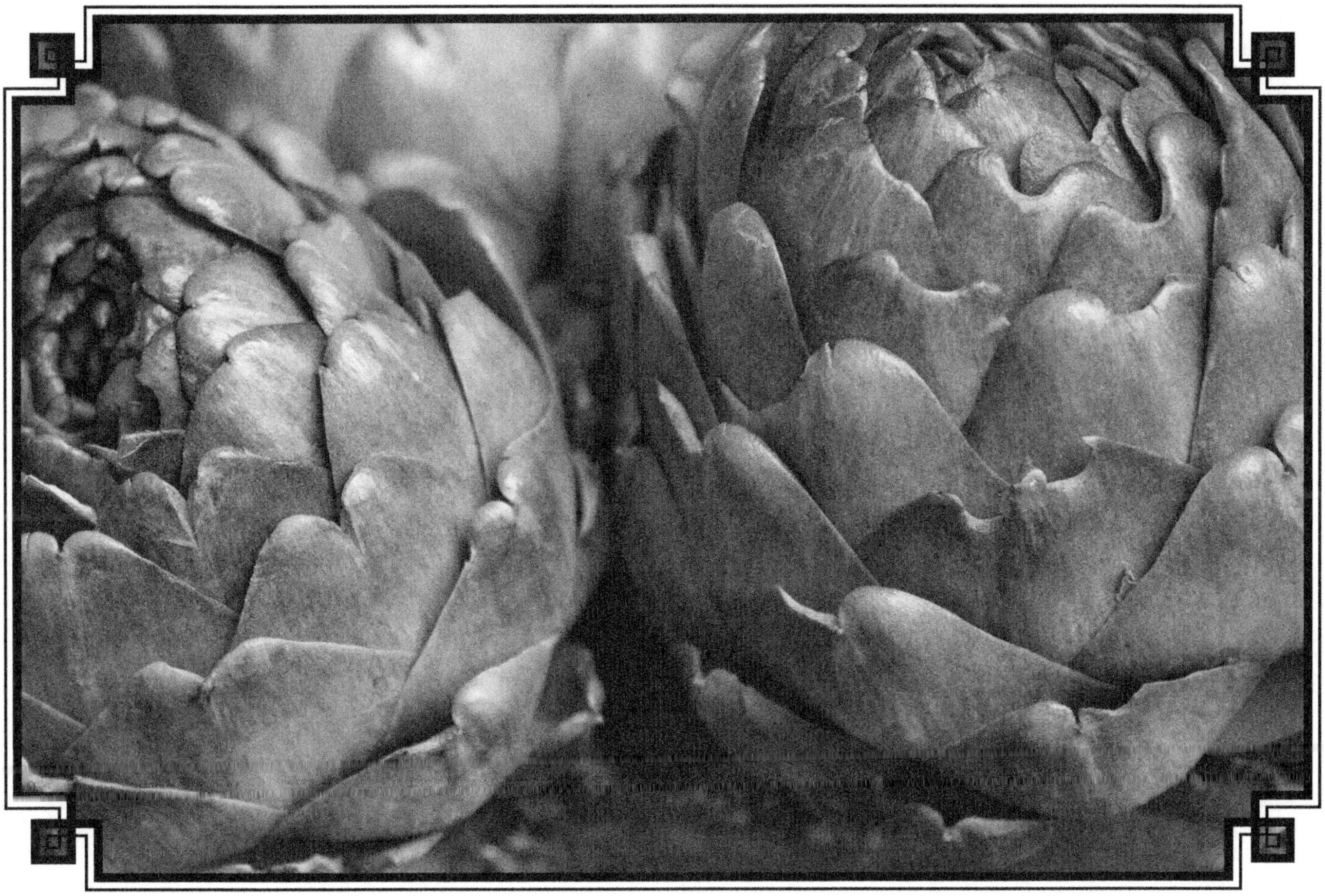

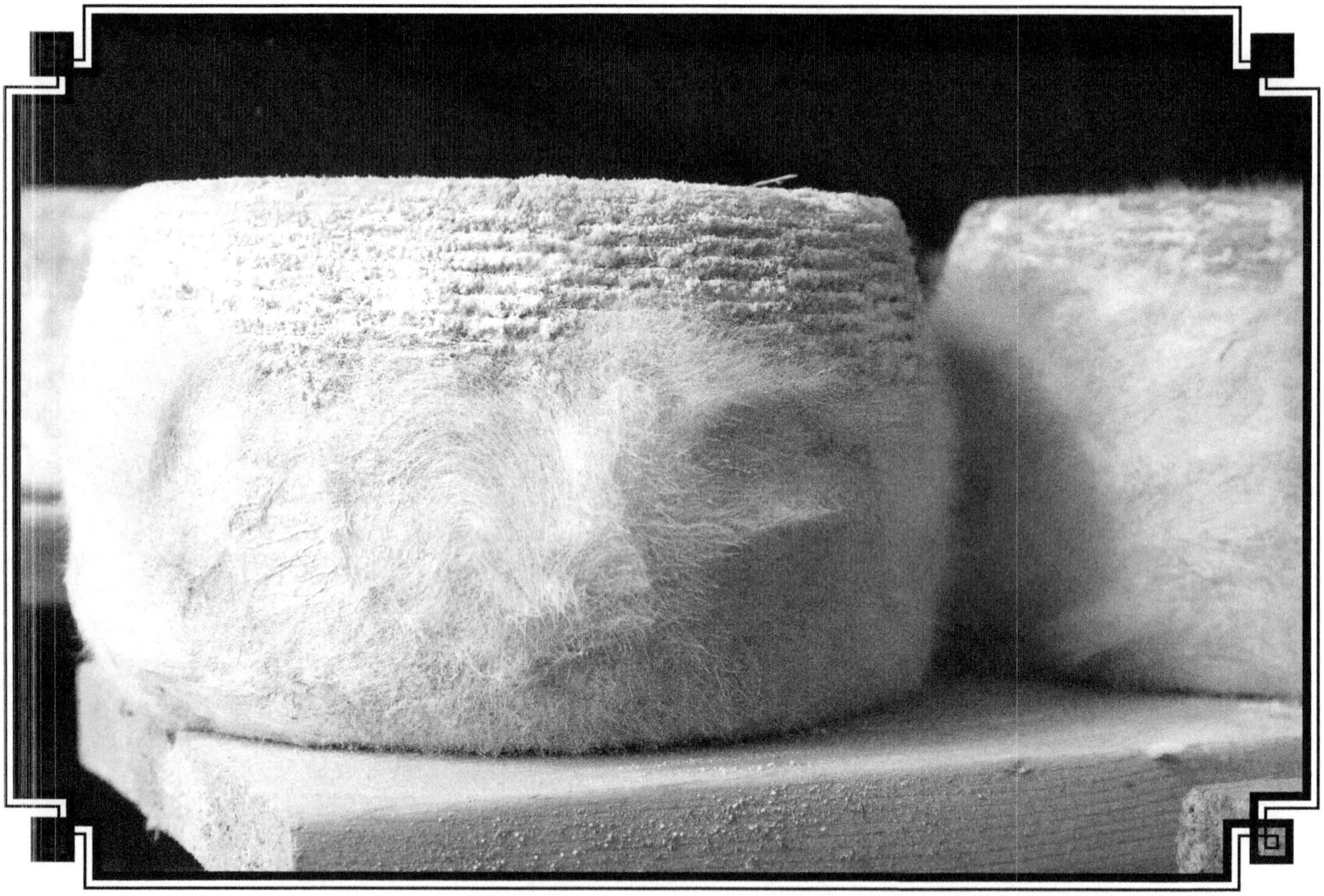

CHEESE BASED RECIPES

Scamorza Witha Sausage

GRILL IT — The Italian Way

Description:

Scamorza is a typical spun paste cheese, mainly produced in the South of Italy. Made of cow milk, it is found in many variants and also smoked. Very good on its own, it is more and more often used together with the ingredients of other dishes - both first and second courses - as well as in Pizzas and Focacce.

Here we propose it as the main protagonist.

Preparation: Easy - Cooking: Fast

What's needed . per people

- Italian Scamorza - The quantity depends on the size. Calculate about 0.45 lb. per person.
- Pure Pork Sausage – 0.11 lb.

How to Prepare

If the scamorzas are small, cut them in half lengthwise, otherwise cut them into rounds about 0.6 in. thick.

Peel the sausages and divide the inside by the number of Scamorza pieces.

Place the scamorza on the grill over moderate heat for a couple of minutes. Turn them over and spread the Sausage pulp over the surface. Leave them like this for another 2 or 3 minutes (be careful not to let the cheese melt too much.

Remove the Scamorze from the grill and serve immediately.

Accompany them with a side of grilled vegetables (see recipe), or with a nice Pinzimonio.

Recommended Wines: Montepulciano d'Abruzzo, or Aglianico del Vulture (Basilicata).

Cheese On Plates

GRILL IT   The Italian Way

Description:

This is certainly not an exclusive preparation of the Mediterranean countries, but in Italy the variety of available cheeses is so great that one would never stop experimenting. I can assure overseas readers that there are literally thousands of them. Obviously, for this type of cooking, the ideal ones are those of medium-soft consistency. E.g. like the famous French Camembert. Very used, in Italy, are the so called "Tomini" made both with goat milk, variously flavored, according to the place of origin, and just cow or mixed milk. But it is impossible in this case, to give a precise indication, because it will depend a lot on what you will be able to find.

Preparation: Quick - Cooking: Quick

What's needed . per person

- Italian soft cheese (Tomini) - about 0.45 lb.
- Extra Virgin Olive Oil (EVO)
- Powdered Thyme
- Ground Pepper
- Salt

- Dried Fruits (Almonds, Walnuts, Hazelnuts) without shell – 0.71 ounce
- Honey (preferably Acacia or Ivy)
- Mix of Fresh Blueberries and Raspberries – 3.5 ounce

How to Prepare

Of course, soak the Cedar Plates in water for about an hour.
Prepare the Cheese, greasing the surface with the Evo Oil. Add a pinch of Salt and Pepper.
The Grill should be set for Direct Cooking at about 370 °F.
Place the Plates on the grill for a couple of minutes, then turn them over and place the cheeses on top. On the top surface put the Blueberry-Raspberry Mix, then pour a little Honey and a pinch of Thyme on top.
Bake for at least 7 to 8 minutes, keeping the lid closed. Halfway through cooking, arrange the dried fruit on the plates.
At the end of cooking, the plates will be served directly to the table and you will be able to enjoy this delight by accompanying it with Honey... and one of the wines we suggest here below.

Suggested Wines: Dry Moscato d'Asti (Piedmont) or Passito di Pantelleria (Sicily) or Muffato (Umbria)

Croutons With Speck, Red Radicchio And Italian Mozzarella

GRILL IT — The Italian Way

Description:

A simple and quick preparation, but very tasty. Speck is a particular type of salami, similar to smoked ham, produced almost exclusively in Trentino Alto Adige, but now widely used in all Italian regions. Mozzarella doesn't need any introduction: it is impossible to get more Italian than this. There are countless varieties, both made of cow's milk and buffalo's milk. The latter gives Mozzarella that unmistakable and inimitable taste which makes it an absolute must of Italian Cooking. Red Radicchio is a valuable variety of the already excellent vegetable but, as opposed to other big leaf vegetables, it is often used together with other foods and in particular, with grilled foods. The most famous and renowned one is Radicchio Rosso di Treviso I.G.P.

Preparation: Quick - Cooking: Quick

What's needed . per person

- At least two slices of Pane Casareccio (the one with the crust, to be clear)
- Italian Mozzarella – 1.6 ounce. For each slice of bread (small Mozzarella are preferable, but thick slices or cubes of larger ones are also acceptable)
- Speck Alto Adige I.G.P. - 2 thin slices for each slice of bread
- Red Radicchio from Treviso I.G.P. - One leaf for each slice of bread
- Extra Virgin Olive Oil (EVO)
- Ground Black Pepper
- Salt

How to Prepare

Start by washing the vegetables and prepare enough leaves for each slice of bread. Dry them well.
Now prepare the Mozzarella (or individual pieces or slices) by wrapping them with the two thin slices of Speck.
Assemble the skewers with the Mozzarella, preferably using steel skewers. If you use wooden skewers, obviously, you will have to wet them first for at least ten minutes.
Cut the individual slices of Pane Casareccio. You can also use Crate Bread... but the result will certainly be more disappointing.

Set your grill for direct cooking at a temperature between 180 and 200 °C.
Now place all the elements (separately) on the grill.
The first to be "cooked" will be the Bread, just as when you prepare Toast. Then remove it from the grill when it is toasted to the right degree for your taste.
Then remove the Radicchio, which you will season with a drizzle of EVO oil, a pinch of Salt and a sprinkling of ground Pepper.
Last, remove the skewers when the Speck has reached a crispy consistency.

Now assemble your Croutons with the Slice of Bread, the Radicchio and one or two Mozzarella & Speck rolls. Enjoy!

Recommended Wines: Gewurztraminer (Alto Adige) or Greece di Tofu (Campania)

Grilled Pecorino Cheese

GRILL IT — The Italian Way

Description:

Pecorino cheese can be found in practically every Italian region, with hundreds of varieties that differ from each other either in the way they are made, or in the way they are aged and refined.
It's also easily available, as it keeps very well and for a long time. Therefore, you're spoilt for choice! Generally, Pecorino is consumed as it is, accompanied by Honey and Fruit Compotes, or as a condiment for other dishes (such as Pasta) but, especially in central Italy, it is also very much appreciated when grilled.

Preparation: Medium - Cooking: Fast

What's needed . per person

- Medium seasoned Pecorino cheese (preferably Roman, Umbrian or Tuscan) - 1 slice about 0.6 in thick.
- Extra Virgin Olive Oil (EVO) – 1.5 oz.
- Oregano
- Mint or Roman mint
- Ground Pepper (Optional)

How to Prepare

Finely chop the Mint and Oregano and pour the mixture into the EVO oil. Place the Pecorino cheese in the flavored oil and leave it season for at least 60 minutes. From time to time turn the cheese to wet it evenly.

Prepare the BBQ for Indirect Cooking at 335 °F and use a well-cleaned and oiled grill. Use the same oil in which you have soaked the cheese.

Place the Pecorino on the grill and after about 5 or 6 minutes turn it over, continuing to brush it with oil. In general, after a total of 10 minutes you can remove the slice and serve immediately.

Recommended Wines: Cesanese del Piglio (Lazio) or Amarone della Valpolicella (Veneto)

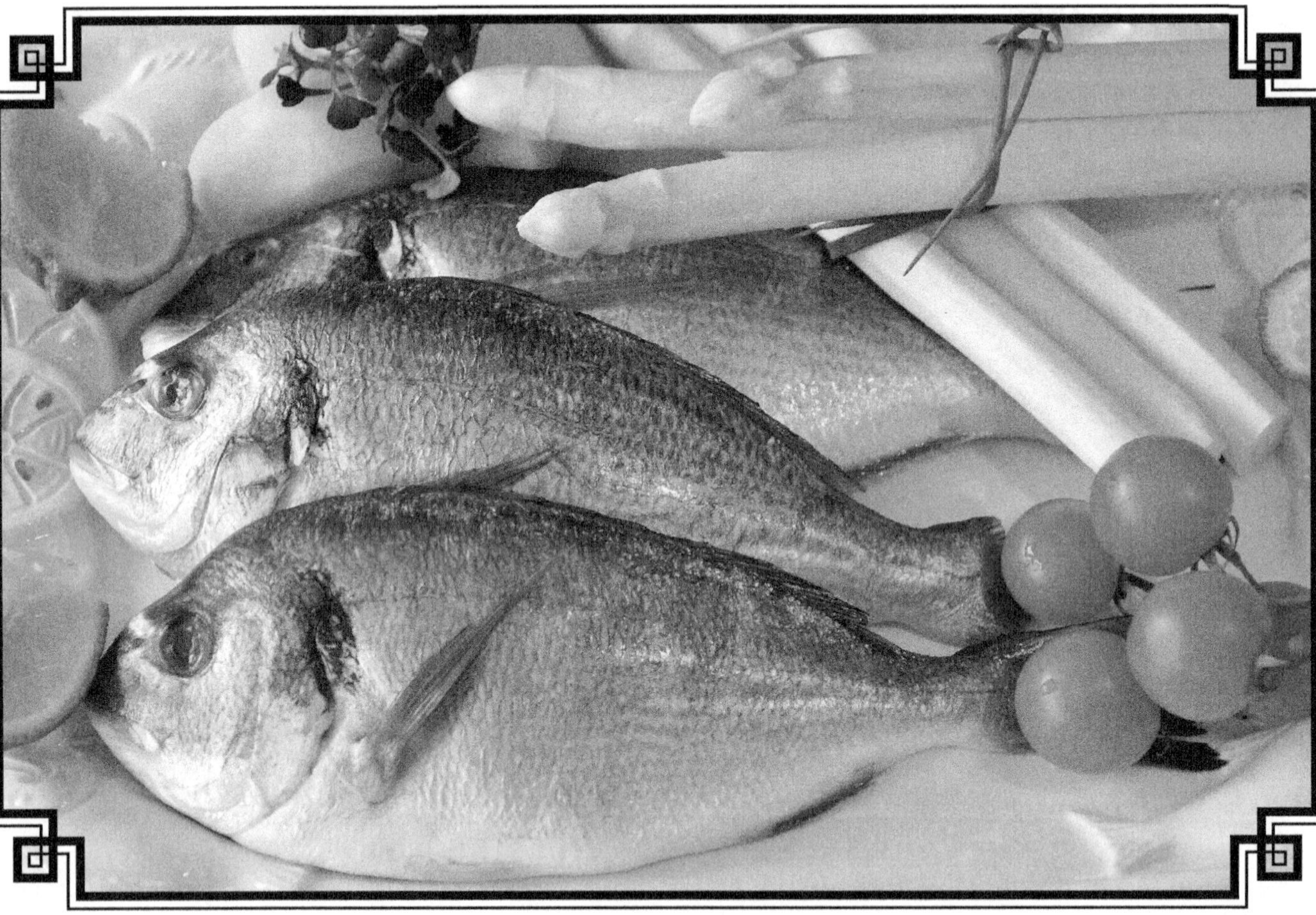

FISH & SEAFOOD RECIPES

Glazed Tuna With Citrus Fruits

GRILL IT — The Italian Way

Description:

Tuna, in its various species, is notoriously a very common and appreciated fish all over the world. Of course, for this preparation the ideal would be a type coming from the Mediterranean but, since the freshness of the slice you are going to use is an essential requirement, you can choose the most easily available type. Once again, the condiments will make the difference.

Preparation: Easy - Cooking: Fast - Cost: Medium

What's needed . per person

- Tuna fillet cut to a minimum thickness of 1.5 in.
- Half a lemon from Sicily or the Amalfi Coast, squeezed. Alternatively, 1 Mandarin.
- Extra Virgin Olive Oil (EVO) – 0.85 oz.
- Balsamic Vinegar – 1 teaspoon
- Acacia Honey - 1 teaspoon
- Mustard - 1 teaspoon
- Chopped Fresh Rosemary - A Pinch
- Salt - One Pinch
- Ground Black Pepper

How to Prepare

Combine all the ingredients (except the Tuna) and mix well until you have a well blended marinating mixture. If the tuna slices are large, you can double the amount.

Once the Marinade is ready, place the Tuna slices in it for half an hour and sprinkle it evenly with the mixture.

Preparation of the Grill:
The grill must be very clean and greased with Olive Oil so that the Tuna meat does not stick. Cooking must take place at a high temperature.

Place the marinated slices on the grill and (if present) close the lid. The cooking time depends mainly on the thickness of the slices, so you will have to adjust by eye, paying attention to the appearance of "Grill Marks" (usually after 2 or 3 minutes). At that point, using a special fish spatula, you can turn the slices over (just once, mind you) and finish cooking. The total cooking time will vary according to taste (always check the temperature with the appropriate thermometer), but we always recommend not to overcook it. In fact, it is the contrast between the delicate flavor of the inner flesh and the caramelized flavor of the outer crust that gives this dish its raison d'être.

Recommended Wines: Sauvignon Blanc (Friuli Venezia Giulia) if you like fragrant wines, or Vermentino di Gallura (Sardinia).

Fish Fillets With Herbs

GRILL IT — The Italian Way

Description:

This recipe is for Fish to be cooked in Steaks. I suggest you try typical Mediterranean fish (you will certainly find frozen fish, especially sea bass and sea bream that may come from fish farms) such as sea bream, sea bass, dentex and seabream, but also more popular fish such as cod or salt cod.

Preparation: Medium - Cooking: Quick

What's needed . per person

- 1 or 2 Fish Fillets (skin on) per Person (depends on size and... hunger)
- Enough Mediterranean herbs to cover a perforated tray to be placed on the grill. Divided as follows: Thyme, Laurel, Sage, Rosemary, Oregano (optional).
- 1 or 2 Sicilian lemons (or Ravello lemons - Amalfi Coast) depending on the number of fillets.
- Extra Virgin Olive Oil (EVO) for seasoning.
- Ground Black Pepper
- Salt.

How to Prepare

Purchase the fish already filleted, or do it yourself if you are able.
Wash the fillets and dry them well. Make slight oblique incisions on the skin side. Dress them with EVO oil, salt and a sprinkling of ground pepper.
Wash the Aromatic Herbs and then leave them in water for 30/40 minutes.
Once dried, gently mix the herbs and place them on a fish tray with holes, together with the sliced lemons.
Place the tray on the grill which has already been prepared for indirect cooking and heated to about 390 °F. If you have a Barbecue with a lid, close it and leave the Herbs inside for 5 minutes.
Now place the fish fillets on the grill with the meat side down (in contact with the herbs) and let them cook for about ten minutes. It is worthwhile to check the state of cooking directly. If you can measure the temperature with a thermometer, the meat is cooked at 150 °F, otherwise, when it becomes white and firm.
Now serve at the table, with a nice Pinzimonio* on the side and, if desired, some Mayonnaise.

Recommended Wines: Vermentino (Tuscany) or Verdicchio dei Castelli di Jesi (Marche).

Shrimps' Skewers

GRILL IT — The Italian Way

Description:

Shrimps, also called Imperial Shrimps, are typical crustaceans of the Mediterranean sea. They are often large in size and have a more refined taste than prawns (which can always be fished in the Mare Nostrum and can also be used in this recipe) and all the other common prawns present in Italy and in all parts of the world. They are easily recognizable because they are lighter in color, grayish or streaked with pink, compared to the more or less intense red of the others.
It is almost superfluous to underline they have a delicious taste even when they are grilled.

Preparation: Medium - Cooking: Fast

What's needed . per person

- At least 4 or 5 Shrimps (or Prawns)
- Extra Virgin Olive Oil (EVO) - 1 Spoonful
- Garlic - 1 clove
- Chopped Dry Chili Pepper (you can substitute with Sweet Paprika Powder if you don't like spicy) - 1 teaspoon tip.
- Ground Black Pepper
- Salt

How to Prepare

Wash and clean the tarts thoroughly. Deprive them of the shell and the head, but leave the tail intact. In an appropriate container (suitable for the quantity of crustaceans) mix carefully the EVO oil, the finely chopped garlic, the chili pepper (or paprika), the salt (do not exaggerate) and a pinch of pepper.
Soak the crustaceans in the marinade, cover the container and refrigerate for an hour.

Prepare the fire for direct cooking over fairly high heat.
Place the shrimps on steel skewers (alternatively, you can use wooden or bamboo skewers, but you will need to soak them in water for half an hour before use).
Place the skewers on the grill and let them cook for a few minutes per side (depending on the size, a variable time between 2 and 5 minutes) until they take on a nice red-orange color, or the internal temperature reaches 140 °F.

Eat the Shrimps accompanied by a simple or garlic flavored mayonnaise and a classical Pinzimonio*.

Suggested Wines: Catarratto (Sicily) or Negroamaro Rosé (Apulia)

Grilled King Prawns

GRILL IT　　　　　　　　　　　　　　　　　　　　　　　The Italian Way

Description:

The spread of these tasty crustaceans is much wider than the Mazzancolle of the previous recipe. Here, in the Mediterranean Sea we have some particularly large and appetizing ones, especially the ones from Gallipoli (Puglia) and Mazzara del Vallo (Sicily).
However, it is possible to find excellent ones almost everywhere, especially those fished in the Atlantic Ocean, in Argentina which reach, frozen, the stores of half the world.
Actually this is a variation of the previous recipe. The differences are in the marinade and in the cooking method, while prawns and shrimps are interchangeable.

Preparation: Medium - Cooking: Fast

What's needed . 4 people

- Red Prawns - At least 4/5 large prawns per person. Alternatively, Shrimps
-
- Extra Virgin Olive Oil (EVO) – 3.5 oz.
- Garlic - 3 Cloves
- Lemons - 2
- Orange - 1
- Fennel Seeds
- Chopped Chilli Pepper
- Salt

How to Prepare

Start by preparing the marinade mixture. Combine the EVO oil with the finely chopped garlic and the grated lemon and orange peel. The lemons and oranges must be chemically untreated. Add the juice of the lemons and orange, a pinch of salt and chili pepper, and a teaspoon of fennel seeds.

After thoroughly cleaning and rinsing the crustaceans, discard the heads and then blot well with kitchen paper.

Now immerse them in the marinating liquid, wetting them well on all sides. Leave them to marinate for 1 or 2 hours in the refrigerator.
Once the marinade is over, the grill must be prepared for direct cooking at a temperature between 360 and 410°F.

The prawns can be placed directly on the grill, or on special trays with holes.

Cooking will be rather quick - on average, 4/5 minutes total, turning only once) - in relation to the size of the crustaceans.

You can accompany these prawns with your favorite sauces but, to remain in the Italian tradition, the ideal will be a Pinzimonio* of raw vegetables.

Recommended Wines: Grechetto (Umbria) or Ribolla Gialla (Friuli Venezia Giulia).

Octopus Salentina Style

GRILL IT — The Italian Way

Description:

Octopus is a staple of Apulian seafood cuisine. They are easily caught on those coasts (even by amateurs, during the summer season) and it is common to see people slamming the octopus on the rocks to soften them. Fresh octopus in fact has a rather "tough" flesh. There are many ways to cook octopus, and grilled octopus is the least common, but not the least deserving. If you do not have fresh octopus, you can still use frozen ones, which will also have the advantage of being already... softened.

Preparation: Quick - Cooking: Medium

What's needed . 4 people

- Octopuses – 2.2 lb.
- Rosemary (fresh if possible)
- Thyme (fresh if possible)
- Parsley (fresh if possible)
- Lemon - 1 (not chemically treated)
- Extra Virgin Olive Oil (EVO) – 3.4 oz.
- Salt
- Black Pepper

How to Prepare

Prepare an emulsion with all the finely chopped herbs, the lemon juice, the EVO oil, a pinch of salt and a pinch of pepper. If the lemon is untreated, you can add its grated rind.

Wash and clean the octopus well, removing the guts and beak. Then, dry them. If the Octopuses are small, between 0.45 and 0.70 lb. Leave them whole, otherwise divide them into two or more parts.

Grease the grill of your Barbecue well with EVO oil. Then place the octopus on it.
They should be cooked over indirect heat, at a temperature between 340 and 375 °F for 35 to 50 minutes, depending on the size of the octopus, which should be turned at least a couple of times. They will be cooked to the right point when the consistency of the meat has become soft.

Once ready, remove them from the grill and dip them in the emulsion.

You can eat them like this, accompanied by boiled potatoes or potatoes cooked directly on the grill, or with a Pinzimonio* of raw vegetables. A typical Salento alternative is to eat the grilled octopus in a sandwich, together with boiled potatoes and a slice of cheese.

Recommended Wines: Primitivo di Manduria Rosè (Puglia) or Falanghina del Sannio (Campania)

Stuffed Squids

GRILL IT The Italian Way

Description:

Here is another recipe that, just hearing its name, cannot help but evoke the Mediterranean Sea! Even at this moment, while I'm writing this on my Laptop, locked up at home in the city... I immediately visualized a restaurant on the seashore, perhaps in the Aeolian Islands, or on the Amalfi Coast, where I could taste this exquisite preparation, in front of amazing landscapes and smelling the intoxicating scents of the Mediterranean scrub. Strong emotions, if experienced live ... but waiting to go there, why not taste them at home?

Preparation: Medium - Cooking: Fast

What's needed . per person

- Medium-large squid - 2
- Tuna in Oil – 1.1 ounce
- Capers (pickled) - 5/10
- Extra Virgin Olive Oil (EVO)
- Thyme
- Parsley
- Salt
- Ground Pepper
- Cassette Bread

How to Prepare

After washing and cleaning the squid thoroughly, leave only the body to fill and set the tentacles aside.

Now prepare a mix with the drained Tuna, the desalted capers (soak them for a few minutes in a cup of cold water, then take them out and rinse them again) a pinch of Thyme and Parsley. Add the squid tentacles cut into small pieces, 1/2 slice of bread soaked in water and well squeezed and then chop everything with the help of a mixer or blender.

Fill the bodies of the Squid well with this mixture and then close the mouth with toothpicks.

Season the prepared squid with Salt, Ground Pepper and EVO Oil to taste.

They will be cooked over direct heat (360 °F) for 12-15 minutes depending on their size. Turn often to avoid burning.

Recommended wines: Inzolia (Sicily) or Furore (Campania)

Sea & Mountain Prawns

GRILL IT — The Italian Way

Description:

For this recipe, which combines the flavors of the earth with those of the sea, you can use prawns, but also shrimps or scampi. This kind of recipe is very successful, because the taste of Porcini Mushrooms (and mushrooms in general) goes very well with the taste of seafood. Mushrooms can be fresh, but frozen ones are also very good.

Preparation: Medium - Cooking: Fast

What's needed . per person

- Fresh or Frozen Porcini Mushrooms (Boletus Edulis) - 2/3 caps per person
- Red Prawns (alternatively, Shrimps or Scampi) - 4/5 per person
- Extra Virgin Olive Oil (EVO) – 0.7 oz.
- Thyme
- Marjoram
- Chervil
- Peppercorns - Either white or black is fine, but also those ready-made mixes with 4/5 different types.
- Salt

How to Prepare

Wash and clean the heads of the Porcini Mushrooms. Dry them on kitchen paper.
Wash and clean the Crustaceans well, removing the heads.
Pour the EVO oil into a bowl and add the aromas (thyme, chervil, marjoram and peppercorns). Let stand for at least an hour.
Prepare the grill for direct cooking, at 340 °F.
Cut the Prawns lengthwise, on the back, and open them.
The Mushroom Heads can be cooked either sliced or whole. In this case, extend the cooking time by a couple of minutes.
Season with the flavored EVO oil, salt and ground pepper.
Place everything on the grill and cook for 4-5 minutes, turning only once.
When cooked, transfer the Prawns and Mushrooms to a tray and drizzle with the flavored EVO oil.

Recommended Wines: Coda di Volpe (Campania) - Roero Arnheis (Piedmont)

Sardines With Mediterranean Herbs

GRILL IT — The Italian Way

Description:

When we talk about sardines, we talk about blue fish and, when we talk about the latter, we especially talk about Southern Italy. A so called "poor" fish because it has always been fished in abundance in the Mediterranean Sea and it has always been (let's say) undervalued by the wealthy clientele. Bluefish has therefore become a fundamental element in the diet of the "poor" who have always been industrious in creating different methods of preparation. Among other things, Science has then demonstrated remarkable nutritional properties beneficial for the metabolism, as these fish are rich in Omega3, Vitamins and other nutrients. Among the most common varieties there are Mackerel, Sardines, Anchovies and Herring, as well as Tuna, Swordfish and Cod.

Preparation: Quick - Cooking: Quick

What's needed . 4 people

- Fresh or frozen sardines – 1.8 lb.
- Extra Virgin Olive Oil (EVO) - 150 ml.
- Garlic - 1 clove
- Lemons - 1
- Thyme
- Parsley
- Rosemary
- Sage
- Salt
- Black Pepper

How to Prepare

First wash and clean the sardines well, removing the guts and heads.
Pat them dry with kitchen paper and place them on a tray.
Mix the three herbs (Thyme, Parsley and Rosemary) chopping them finely, with a pinch of Salt and a sprinkling of ground Black Pepper.
Dip the individual sardines, first on one side and then on the other, in the mix you have just prepared. Let stand at least 15 minutes.
Meanwhile, in a bowl, combine the EVO oil with the finely chopped garlic and parsley, a pinch of salt and ground pepper. Mix well and add a little lemon juice.
Place the sardines on the grill (direct cooking at 360 °F) for no more than 5 minutes in total, turning once.
Remove the sardines from the grill, place them on a tray and season them generously with the EVO Oil and Spice Mix.

Recommended Wines: Cerasuolo d'Abruzzo Rosè, or Catarratto (Sicily).

Mediterranean Fish (Whole)

GRILL IT — The Italian Way

Description:

I have preferred to bring together in this recipe all the main types of "Precious" Mediterranean Fish of medium size, to be cooked whole. They are all very common and some are even bred in large quantities. I'm mainly talking about Bream and Sea Bass, but also Dentex, Saragus, Mormora and the like. To grill them, they can also be good frozen. Therefore they can be used all over the world. Obviously they differ from each other, but they have in common a delicious taste and have firm and not too spiny meat.

Preparation: Quick - Cooking: Quick

What's needed . per person

- Whole Mediterranean fish – 0.9 lb. (Larger sizes are indicated for more people)
- Extra Virgin Olive Oil (EVO)
- Parsley
- Sage
- Dill
- Rosemary
- Thyme
- Marjoram
- Garlic - 1 clove
- Salt
- Black Pepper
- Lemons - ½ (preferably from Sicily or the Amalfi Coast)

How to Prepare

If you have not purchased them already cleaned, you will need to wash and clean each fish thoroughly, remove the guts and main fins (dorsal, ventral and pectoral) while keeping the fish whole and with the head. Dry them very well. If the fish weigh more than 0.7/0.9 lb. make two oblique incisions with a sharp knife on each side, in the most fleshy areas.

Prepare a mix with all the finely chopped spices and put plenty of them inside each fish. Add a few slices of lemon. Grease the outer surfaces with plenty of EVO oil.

Prepare your Barbecue for direct cooking at a temperature between 340 and 390 °F depending on the size of the fish. The grill should be very clean and should be greased, once slightly heated, with plenty of EVO oil to prevent the skin from sticking. Alternatively, you can use a special accessory for cooking fish.

Place the fish to cook with the lid closed, turning it at two thirds of the cooking time. As an indication, after 7/8 minutes for fish weighing up to 1.1 lb. and after 10 minutes for fish weighing up to 2.2 lb.

GRILL IT — The Italian Way

Cooking will end when the temperature of the fish reaches 150 °F in the fleshiest part. Accompany the fish thus cooked with a mayonnaise-based sauce, and a Pinzimonio* of vegetables, or with potatoes prepared as you like (boiled, grilled, barbecued). No French fries please!

Recommended Wines: Vernaccia di San Gimignano (Tuscany) or Vermentino (Tuscany/Sardinia).

Honey Marinated Shrimps

GRILL IT — The Italian Way

Description:

As in previous recipes, you can use frozen Shrimps, Scampi or Mediterranean Red Prawns, but also fresh Prawns which are easier to find in your area.

Preparation: Medium - Cooking: Fast

What's needed . 4 people

- Shrimps - at least 20
- Extra Virgin Olive Oil – 3.4 oz.
- Fluid Honey (Acacia is ideal) – 6.8 oz.
- Lemon Juice (from Sicily or the Amalfi Coast) – 1.7 oz.
- Brown Sugar – 1 teaspoon
- Thyme or Oregano
- Salt

How to Prepare

Clean and wash the crustaceans well. Remove guts and heads. Dry them well.
Now prepare a Marinate by mixing together the other ingredients.
Immerse the crustaceans in the liquid thus prepared, covering all surfaces.
Let everything rest for at least one hour.

Prepare the Barbecue for direct cooking at a temperature of about 370 °F and then arrange the Crustaceans on the Grill. The maximum cooking time will be about 10 minutes, but check yourself that they do not burn. Brush the surfaces with the remaining marinade on one side at the beginning and the other halfway through cooking.

A nice fresh salad with cherry tomatoes or Datterini di Pachino, or a Pinzimonio* will be the ideal side dish.

Recommended Wines: Passerina (Abruzzo) or Vermentino (Tuscany)

Eel Or Capitone (Female Eel)

GRILL IT — *The Italian Way*

Description:

Here is a preparation closely tied to the Christmas season, especially in Southern Italy - so much so that it also appeared in Eduardo de Filippo's theatrical masterpiece "Natale in Casa Cupiello". Like many recipes, a marinating will be necessary before cooking.

Preparation: Medium - Cooking: Fast

What's needed . 4 people

- Eel (or Capitone) – 0.5 lb. per person
- Extra Virgin Olive Oil (EVO)
- Wine Vinegar
- Bay Leaves (Optional)
- Garlic - 3 or 4 Cloves
- Salt
- Black Pepper

How to Prepare

Wash and clean the Eel (or Capitone) well and then cut it into pieces no more than 8 cm long.
Rub each piece with the garlic cloves, peeled and cut in two, on the side of the cut.
Place them on a tray, then season with the EVO Oil, a splash of Wine Vinegar, Salt, Ground Pepper and the finely chopped Garlic. Turn each piece well and then leave to marinate for a couple of hours.
Now prepare the individual skewers (metal ones are best) alternating the pieces of eel with the bay leaves.
Set up the BBQ at a temperature of about 300 - 320 °F for direct cooking.
Generally, these skewers cook in about 30 - 40 minutes, taking care to turn them often and to grease them several times with EVO oil, applied with a sprig of rosemary.

Recommended Wines: Vernaccia di San Gimignano (Tuscany) or Pecorino (Abruzzo)

Tuna Meatballs On Cedar Plate

GRILL IT — *The Italian Way*

Description:
This is a recipe to immediately make a good impression right from the appetizer. In fact it is very tasty and you will see that, like cherries... one leads to another. The secret lies in the use of Parmesan cheese in addition to the already tasty tuna. A possible alternative, is the use of olive wood plates, instead of those of Cedar.

Preparation: Quick - Cooking: Quick

What's needed. 4 people

- Tuna in Oil – 0.88 lb.
- Parmiggiano Reggiano D.O.P. (Alternatively, Grana Padano D.O.P. - DO NOT use Parmesan Cheese) – 0.55 lb.
- Fresh Eggs - 2
- Milk - 250 ml.
- Crate Bread - 3 slices
- Dry Bread (or Grated Bread) – 0.55 lb.
- Potatoes – 0.55 - 0.9 lb.
- Garlic - 1 clove
- Parsley
- Extra Virgin Olive Oil (EVO)
- Salt,
- Ground Pepper

How to Prepare

Combine the following elements in an appropriate container: Tuna, well drained - Potatoes, after boiling and mashed - Cassette bread softened in milk - Egg yolks - Finely chopped garlic and parsley - Salt and pepper to taste. Knead everything well until it reaches a consistency that is not too soft, but homogeneous.

Now cut the Parmesan cheese (or Grana cheese) into many pieces, which will then be inserted into the meatballs. Form with your hands some meatballs (round or a bit squashed depending on how you prefer them) with a maximum diameter of 1.5 in. Insert a piece of Parmiggiano in the middle.

Dip the meatballs in the dry breadcrumbs and grease them with EVO oil.

While you are soaking the Wooden Planks in warm water (at least 30 minutes) start the Barbecue, setting it to a temperature of about 375 °F and Indirect Cooking.

Now place the patties on the plates and place them directly over the grill until the plates begin to smoke. Then, move them to the Indirect Cooking area. The total cooking time will be between 18 and 25 minutes, depending on your taste.

Allow the meatballs to cool slightly before serving at the table and accompany them with Garlic Flavored Mayonnaise.

Recommended Wines: Grechetto (Umbria) or Chardonnay (Sicily).

Scallops Land 'n Sea

GRILL IT The Italian Way

Description:

Seafood with a particularly refined taste, which also lend themselves (thanks to their beautiful shells) to elegant presentations. In this version, I propose them with two important elements of Italian cuisine: both land Prosciutto Crudo (Raw Ham) and, we could say, sea... since Pesto was born in Liguria, by the sea.

Preparation: Quick - Cooking: Quick

What's needed . per person

- Fresh Scallops - 4
- Extra Virgin Olive Oil (EVO) – 0.53 oz.
- Fresh Basil – 1.6 ounce.
- Toasted Pine Nuts – 0.8 ounce.
- Garlic - ½ clove
- Lemon - 1 teaspoon juice
- D.O.P. Parma Ham - 1 slice, not too thin
- Salt
- Ground Pepper

How to Prepare

Rinse the scallops and set the shells aside. Then dry them well.
Now you will need to prepare the Pesto.
Use a blender where you will put the Basil, Pine Nuts, Garlic, Lemon juice, a pinch of Salt and Pepper. Blend everything well and then slowly add (while continuing to blend) the EVO oil. Everything should have a creamy consistency.
Now divide each slice of Prosciutto into 4 parts and wrap a Scallop in each of them. Secure the ham using a toothpick.
Spread the Pesto in each scallop shell.

Set your BBQ for direct cooking at about 300 °F. Clean and oil the grill, then arrange the Scallops on it. Keep an eye on the ham and prevent it from toasting too much. As a guideline, 4 to 6 minutes are enough.
Remove everything and place the Scallops in their respective shells, on the bed formed by the Pesto. I have to say that, just writing this... I already envy you!

Recommended Wines: Pigato (Liguria) or Sauvignon Blanc (Friuli Venezia Giulia)

Sliced Fish

GRILL IT — The Italian Way

Description:

From Cod, spread practically all over the world, to the tastiest Mediterranean fish (often available from fish farms or frozen) such as Sea Bass, Gilthead Seabream, Dentex, Seabream and many others, what could be better than a flavorful grilled fish? In this case, we will use only the fillets (or slices)

Preparation: Medium - Cooking: Fast

What's needed . per person

- Marine Fish - 1 of at least 0.88 lb. - Alternatively, 2 fillets already cut and cleaned
- Garlic - 1 clove
- Lemon of Sicily or the Amalfi Coast
- Parsley
- Thyme
- Extra Virgin Olive Oil (EVO) – 1.5 oz.
- Ground Pepper
- Salt

How to Prepare

First wash and clean the fish well, then cut two fillets.
Then, in a bowl of appropriate size, mix well the EVO oil with chopped Parsley, Thyme and Garlic together with the juice of half a Lemon. Season with salt and pepper.
Immerse the fillets in the liquid and let them marinate for at least an hour and a half.

Prepare your Grill for Direct Cooking, at a temperature of about 340 °F. Clean the grill well and oil it thoroughly to avoid adhering the skin of the fish.

Now place the well drained fillets on the grill with the skin in contact with it. The fish should be placed transversely to the metal rods and not parallel.

Let them cook for 5 or 6 minutes, brushing occasionally with the marinating liquid. At this point, carefully turn them over and leave that way for another 2 minutes.

Now you can serve them at the table, accompanied by slices of lemon and a side dish of vegetables of your choice, although I strongly advise against French fries.

Recommended Wines: Catarratto (Sicily) or Vermentino (Sardinia)

BBQ Mussels

GRILL IT — The Italian Way

Description:

An irreplaceable element in Italian seafood cuisine, mussels are found in many countries and seas. Of course, if Taranto's mussels are available… then we are really at the top! They are prepared in a thousand different ways, but the one on the BBQ is definitely less common. This does not make it any less interesting or tasty, as cooking them on the grill will give a smoky flavor to these already tasty mussels that will certainly give them an extra kick.

Preparation: Quick - Cooking: Quick

What's needed . 4 people

- Mussels (preferably Italian, from Taranto) – 3.4 lb.
- Extra Virgin Olive Oil (EVO)
- Garlic - 2 Cloves
- Parsley
- Sicilian Lemons
- Ground Pepper

How to Prepare

Wash the mussels well and then dry them.
Place them directly on the BBQ using a grill or a cast iron griddle. The setting and temperature are not important, because there is an unmistakable sign that the cooking is finished: the opening of the shells. At that point, remove the mussels and season them with EVO oil, a pinch of ground pepper, chopped garlic & parsley. If you wish, add a few drops of lemon juice.

Recommended Wines: Negramaro Rosé (Puglia) – Cerasuolo Rosè (Abruzzo)

Mackerel With Mediterranean Salad

GRILL IT — The Italian Way

Description:

I have already talked about this (and other) important representative of the so-called Blue Fish. Very common, especially in the Mediterranean and in the North Atlantic, it is also known as „Sgombro". Rich in Omega 3, it is therefore not only tasty, but healthy too. Let yourself be tempted by a rich grill with this magnificent fish, accompanied by the typical Mediterranean flavors.

Preparation: Quick - Cooking: Quick

What's needed. 4 people

- Mackerel (fresh) - 1 or 2 per person (depending on size)
- Extra Virgin Olive Oil (EVO)
- Mandarins - 1 per person
- Fennel - 2
- Fresh Spearmint or Roman mint (Mentuccia Romana)
- Ground Pepper
- Salt

How to Prepare

The first thing to do is to wash and clean the fish well. Then dry them with kitchen paper. Now grease each one with EVO oil.

Set the BBQ for direct cooking at 340 °F and use a clean grill or a cast iron plate, well greased with EVO oil.

Cook the fish for a total of 18 - 22 minutes, basting occasionally with EVO oil, and turn them over after about 10 minutes.

Prepare a separate salad with diced Fennel and Mandarin segments and dress with EVO Oil, Fresh Roman Mint, Salt and Pepper.

Now you can serve at the table and enjoy a really tasty dish.

Recommended Wines: Malvasia Puntinata (Lazio) or Grechetto (Umbria)

Mediterranean Fish Baked In Foil

GRILL IT | The Italian Way

Description:
Take them frozen, but take Mediterranean fish for this recipe. A nice sea bream, a sea bass, a dentex or a seabream are ideal for the preparation of "Cartoccio". Here all the aromas, scents and flavors of the Mediterranean will literally explode, delighting your palate and that of your (envious) guests.

Preparation: Easy - Cooking: Quick

What's needed . per person

- Mediterranean Fish - 1 of about 0.9 lb (Bream, Sea Bass, Dentex, Seabream, Pagello and similar)
- Extra Virgin Olive Oil (EVO)
- Sicilian Orange – one half
- Oregano
- Thyme
- Parsley
- Mint
- Salt
- Ground Black Pepper

How to Prepare

After having thoroughly washed and cleaned the fish, prepare a mixture with the listed flavors, salt and pepper to taste and mix it with plenty of EVO oil. Grease the skin well and pour a little bit inside the fish too.

Make a couple of oblique cuts in the skin of the Fish on both sides.

For each fish at your disposal, use a sheet of aluminum foil, which you will also grease with EVO oil. Place a single fish on top of each sheet of aluminum foil, accompanied by a generous amount of the mixture made with the spices and EVO oil.

Carefully close each Cartoccio and place it on your grill, already prepared for direct cooking at 360 °F.

After 10 - 12 minutes, turn the Cartocci over and continue cooking for another 10 minutes.

Serve the open Cartocci (in which you'll squeeze some orange juice) directly on the plates and enjoy the amazed look of your guests!

Recommended Wines: Verdicchio dei Castelli di Jesi (Marche) or Falanghina del Sannio (Campania)

Astice* Or Lobster On Basil

GRILL IT — The Italian Way

Description:

I am perfectly aware that I am "risking my life" here... In fact, when it comes to large Crustaceans, such as Lobster, to be grilled, the North American Tradition (deservedly) is the leader. What I am proposing here is therefore more of a particular condiment (of Mediterranean origin) to test and see if it suits your tastes, so that you can use it to surprise your guests.

Preparation: Quick - Cooking: Quick

What's needed . per person

- Lobster (small to medium size) or European lobster - 1
- Basil Flavored EVO Oil
- Lemons (untreated) from Sicily or the Amalfi Coast
- Fresh Basil

How to Prepare

If you could not find the ready-made Basil Flavored Oil, you will have to prepare it a couple of weeks before. In this case, use an 8.5 oz green glass bottle. Pour in the bottle the Extra Virgin Olive Oil (EVO) together with some fresh basil leaves (well cleaned, washed and dried). Close hermetically and leave to rest away from sources of light and heat.

Take the Lobsters, cut them in half and grease them generously with the Aromatized Oil, then cook them on the Grill in the way that "YOU" know.

Once cooked, season the Crustaceans with a drizzle of EVO oil, a few leaves of fresh basil and grated lemon zest.

Accompany with vegetables of your choice and a some mayonnaise. Very suitable are new potatoes, carrots, or the classic Pinzimonio*.

Recommended Wines: Vermentino (Tuscany) or white Amalfi Coast (Campania)

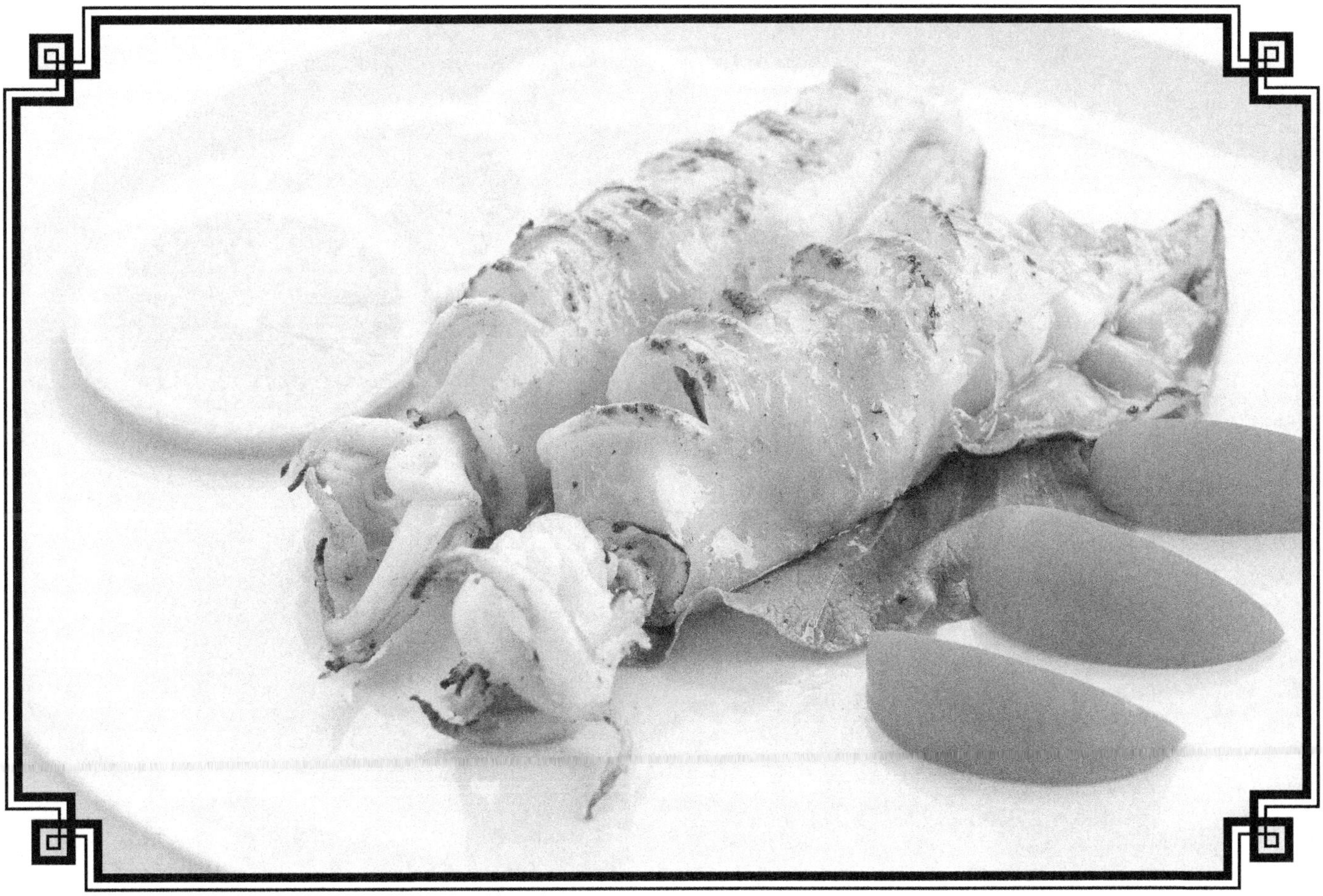

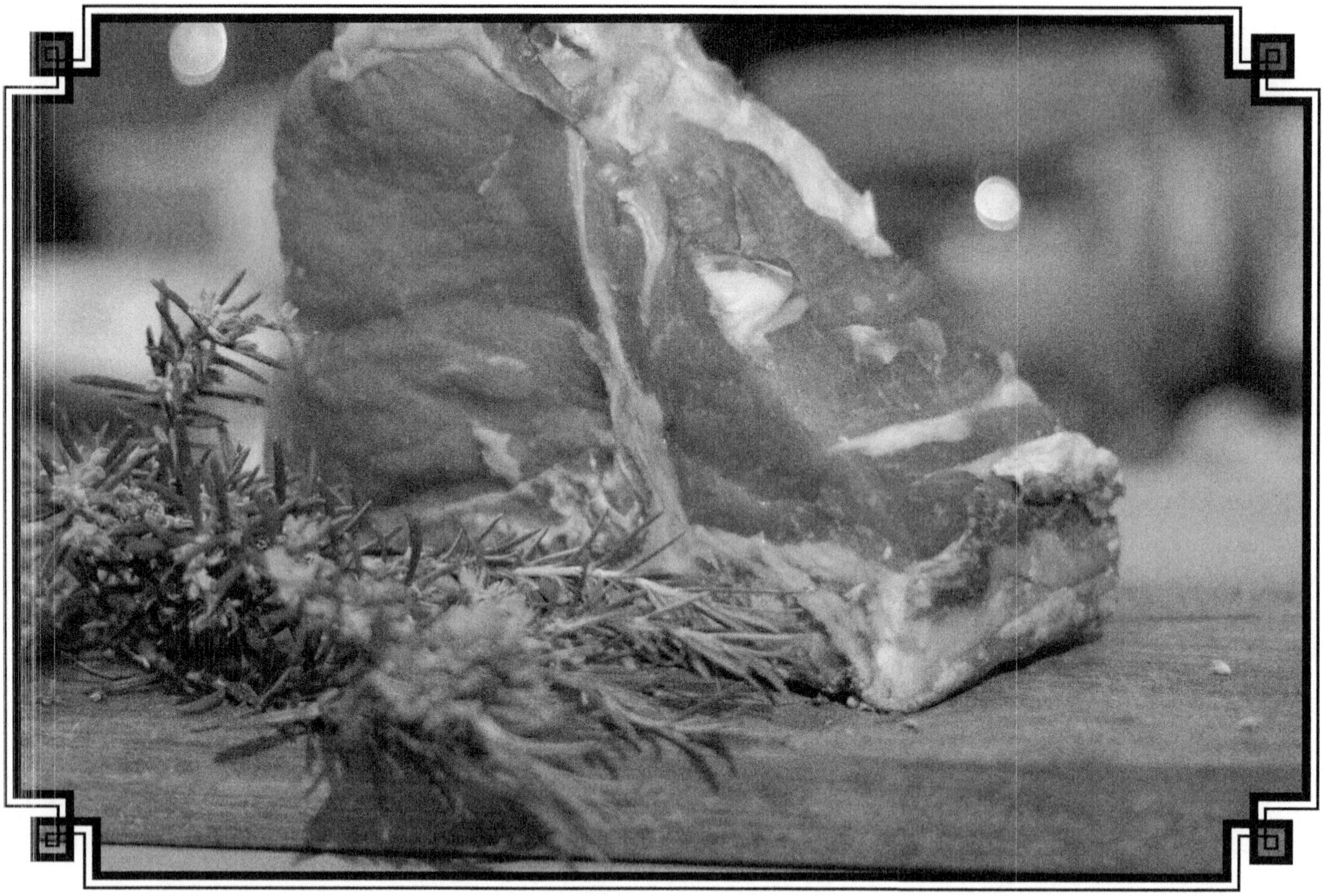

MEAT RECIPES

Lamb's Ribs

GRILL IT — The Italian Way

Description:

Lamb meat is frequently used in the Italian Cooking, especially in the Easter period when, by tradition and prepared in many different ways, lamb cannot be missing in the tables of Italians. It is a custom mainly valid in the center and in the south, as secular traditions of sheep farming and breeding have made the use of this tasty meat very common.

Preparation: Medium - Cooking: Fast

What's needed . 4 people

- Lamb chops - At least 3 or 4 chops per person.

For the preparation

- Extra Virgin Olive Oil (EVO) – 3.4 oz.
- Balsamic Vinegar – 3.4 oz.

- Garlic - 2 Cloves
- Fresh Rosemary - 2 Sprigs (alternatively, but less flavorful, Dried Rosemary – 0.18 ounce.)
- Salt
- Black Pepper

How to Prepare

Wash and clean the lamb chops. If you have purchased a whole loin, separate the individual ribs. Pat dry with kitchen paper.

Prepare a marinade by mixing the EVO oil, balsamic vinegar, rosemary needles (clean and wash if fresh), finely chopped garlic, two pinches of salt and a sprinkling of ground black pepper.

Arrange the chops on a suitable tray and brush them generously with the marinade on all sides. Let stand for at least 3 hours.

In the meantime, prepare the grill or BBQ for indirect heat cooking and bring it to a temperature of about 390 °F.

Cook the ribs, turning occasionally and brushing them with the marinade. This type of meat should be cooked until the internal temperature reaches 150 °F.

Recommended Wines: Cesanese del Piglio (Lazio) or Cannonau (Sardinia).

Lamb's Leg

GRILL IT — The Italian Way

Description:
The leg of lamb (and the shoulder, to a lesser extent) offers a greater quantity of meat compared to the chops and therefore the cooking times are longer, but the preparation and methods remain the same. To vary a little, we have simply changed the type of marinating.

Preparation: Fast - Cooking: Medium

What's needed.

Leg of lamb - generally, a small leg (or shoulder) is enough for 2 people. With larger ones you can reach 3.

For the Preparation

- Extra Virgin Olive Oil (EVO) – 6.8 oz.
- Garlic - 4 cloves to be finely chopped
- Mustard - Preferably Dijon mustard - 4 tablespoonfuls
- Lemons - Ravello or Sicilian lemons preferred - 2
- Fresh Rosemary - As a variation you can try Thyme - 2 bunches
- Black Pepper
- Salt

How to Prepare

First clean and wash the leg (or shoulder) and then remove any excess fat.
Make some incisions in the meat, both horizontally and vertically.

In a special container, mix the Slather ingredients.
Massage the meat with Salt and Ground Black Pepper.

Place the Leg on the Grill (Indirect Cooking, temperature between 360 and 410 °F) and leave it with the lid closed for at least 20 minutes.

Now start brushing the meat every 15' with the Slather, and turn it each time, until the internal temperature has reached 150 °F and the cooking is finished.

Remove the lamb from the grill and leave it to cool for 10 minutes.

Recommended Wines: Morellino di Scansano (Tuscany) or Primitivo di Manduria (Puglia).

Tuscan Rotisserie (Rosticciana)

GRILL IT — The Italian Way

Description:

When we talk about Rosticciana, we are referring to Grilled Pork Ribs, prepared according to the Tuscan custom, which is one of the most popular and appetizing variants.

The choice of the type of cut, the preparation and the type of cooking will strongly influence the results. In Tuscany, in particular, some varieties of pigs are bred particularly valuable, among which the Cinta Senese pig stands out.

Preparation: Medium - Cooking: Medium

What's needed . 4 people

- Half a pork rib - It is important to choose a cut that is as close as possible to the sternum. The so-called "Saint Louis cut". The thickness must be at least 2 inches.
- Sage – 0.35 ounce dried
- Rosemary - 0.35 ounce dried
- Extra Virgin Olive Oil (EVO) – 3.4 oz.
- Garlic - 2 cloves
- Black Pepper
- Salt

How to Prepare

Clean and wash the meat well, removing any excess fat and the membrane on the side opposite the meaty part. DO NOT split the individual chops.

Combine Sage, Rosemary, finely chopped Garlic, Salt to taste and a sprinkling of ground Black Pepper to form a mixture with which you will massage the Carrè Ribs after having generously greased them with EVO Oil.

The cooking of the Rosticciana involves two phases: the first, shorter, carried out at high temperature in a direct way, and the second, longer, to be carried out at indirect heat. First with the meat towards the grill and then on the other side. Close the lid in case you are using a BBQ.

The first phase ends when you see the crust formed on the surface is evenly distributed and not burnt.

At this point, the meat should be moved away from the heat form, with the meat facing upwards, and cooking can continue for at least 60 minutes (with the lid closed in the BBQ). Check with a fork that the meat is tender, firm and easily pierced. The internal temperature should be between 158 and 165 °F depending on how you prefer the cooking.

Recommended Wines: Vino Nobile di Montepulciano (Tuscany) or Brunello di Montalcino (Tuscany)

Pork Loin (Arista) With Mediterranean Herbs

GRILL IT The Italian Way

Description:

Pork loin (otherwise known as Lonza or Capocollo) is a fine cut of the most "eclectic" animal in the world in a gastronomic sense. It can be prepared in many ways, all equally tasty, but in this case I obviously propose the version to be done on the grill, which certainly does not disfigure in front of the others, indeed... For an excellent result, a good preparation of the meat and the right cooking technique are essential. The important thing is... not to be in a hurry.

Preparation: Long - Cooking: Long

What's needed . 4 or 5 people

- Pork Loin (Arista) – 2.2 lb. or more

For the preparation
- Extra Virgin Olive Oil (EVO) – 5.7 oz.
- Garlic powder
- Chopped dried chili pepper
- Onion powder
- Black pepper (you can also experiment with different pepper mixes) ground
- Sweet Paprika powder
- Brown sugar
- Salt
- Garlic - 4 or 5 cloves
- Fresh oregano (alternatively powdered)
- Fresh thyme (or powdered thyme)
- Fresh sage (alternatively powdered)
- Rosemary (alternatively also powdered)

How to Prepare

It is advisable to start the preparation the day before, so that the marinade will flavor the meat as much as possible.

First, wash and clean the Arista well, then dry it thoroughly.

Prepare a mix with the Spices indicated as "powdered", the Cane Sugar and the Salt, to obtain the rub with which to massage the meat.

Separately, combine about 4.7 oz. EVO oil with a mixture of all the other spices. Mix well until you get a creamy consistency.

Next, cut the surface of the Arista into diamond shapes, then coat it with the remaining EVO oil. Now massage it thoroughly with the Rub Mix.
Once this is done, spread the creamy mixture with the chopped herbs over the entire surface. Refrigerate overnight in a closed container or in a freezer bag.

GRILL IT — The Italian Way

The next day the barbecue must have been prepared (well in advance of the meal) for Indirect Cooking, at a temperature no higher than 250 °F. If you wish, you can also use die bricks for flavoring as you like, but I (at least the first time) suggest you try it without, just to fully enjoy the taste given by the Mediterranean herbs.

Take the meat out of the refrigerator at least 90 minutes before cooking.

The meat will be cooked with the lid closed for at least 4 hours (or more in the case of larger cuts) and about 3 hours if the cut is smaller than 1.5 lb.. Turn the meat every half hour and check the internal temperature with a thermometer. When the temperature reaches 150 °F the cooking process is complete.

Serve at the table in large slices with a side dish of your choice. The ideal are potatoes roasted whole and with their skin on the grill, inside an aluminum foil, but on this... I don't pretend to give advice to those who are masters on the subject.

Recommended Wines: Aglianico del Vulture (Basilicata) or Barbaresco (Piedmont)

Cheeseburger With Fontina Valdostana Cheese & Tropea Onions

GRILL IT — The Italian Way

Description:

Don't worry... I'm not swearing. You can prepare the burgers as you like and I won't even give you the ingredients. I will not allow myself...
I will only talk about the "condiment" that will accompany the meat. What characterizes this recipe is in fact the Tropea Onion first of all, but also the Cheese: the Fontina Valdostana in fact has a very particular taste and "smell" (don't be scared by... the taste's very good).

Preparation: Medium - Cooking: Fast

What's needed . per person

- Fontina Valdostana - For each Hamburger. 1 slice not thicker than ¼ in. Alternatively (or in addition), you can make it into many small pieces and mix it with the minced meat during the preparation. Add a drizzle of EVO oil.
- Extra virgin olive oil (EVO)
- Salt

- Red Onions from Tropea (alternatively, Onions from Acquaviva delle Fonti) - At least one, medium-large for each Hamburger
- Brown Sugar - 2 teaspoon
- Wine Vinegar – 0.17 oz.
- Balsamic Vinegar of Modena
- Hamburger Bun

How to Prepare

In a saucepan, heat the Brown Sugar and Wine Vinegar. When the Sugar has dissolved, add the thinly sliced Tropea Onion. Stir continuously, until completely caramelized. Usually, 7 - 8 minutes are enough.

Obviously we are not going to tell you how to prepare the grill or how to cook the burgers. We personally prefer them not overcooked. Just add a slice of Fontina Valdostana on top of each burger a couple of minutes before the end of cooking.

When cooked, place a little bit of Caramelized Onion on the bun, then the Hamburger with Fontina and again a little bit of Onion. Add, if you like, a drop of Balsamic Vinegar of Modena.

I'm sure of one thing... Your neighbors (full of envy) will elect you "King of the Neighborhood". Because they will also be experts on hamburgers... but most of them have never even heard of the other ingredients. You, the readers, on the other hand... YES!

Recommended Wines: NO, forget it... With the Hamburger, Beer is a must!

Bologna's Mortadella

GRILL IT — The Italian Way

Description:

This typically Italian salami (we talked about it at the beginning of this book) is another element with which you can surprise your friends and relatives. It is delicious eaten alone, in thin or thicker slices. In our area, it is a must eat, together with fresh figs, inside a white focaccia cut.
However, it is just as tasty if prepared on the grill.

Preparation: Quick - Cooking: Quick

What's needed. per person

- Mortadella di Bologna I.G.P. - 1 whole slice, cut thick, at least 1.4 in.
- Balsamic Vinegar of Modena

How to Prepare

Prepare the Barbecue for Direct Cooking, at a temperature between 360 and 390 °F and place the slices of Mortadella on the grill for a few minutes, until the dark marks of the grill are evident, then turn it gently and repeat the operation.

Once cooked, remove the slice from the heat and let it cool slightly. Then cut it into cubes and place them in a bowl. Pour a thin layer of balsamic vinegar on top. Let it rest for 2-3 minutes and then serve as an Antipasto (Appetizer).

Recommended Wines: Lambrusco di Sorbara, dry or even sweet (Emilia Romagna) or Sangiovese (Emilia Romagna).

Arrosticini (Sheep Skewers)

GRILL IT — The Italian Way

Description:

This recipe is truly one of the pillars of Italian grilled cuisine. Included in the common Mediterranean tradition of grilled skewers, Arrosticini originated in Abruzzo, a region with an ancient tradition of sheep farming and are made with the meat of sheep. This can be more or less young because, as in every respectable Italian tradition, the "nuances" about what and how it should be prepared vary in every single little town and in every family. But, in substance, some fundamental points always remain the same. Namely, the quality of the meat and the need for an accurate cooking.

For an optimal preparation of arrosticini it will be necessary to use a special grill for skewers (Skewer Cooker) called "Fornacella". This is because the skewers used to cook the meat must be made of wood and not metal. You can buy the Arrosticini ready-made, or (much better) you can make them yourself.

Preparation: Fast - Cooking: Fast

What's needed . per person

- Arrosticini already prepared - At least 10
- Or (to prepare them yourself): Sheep Meat (Lamb, Mutton or Adult Sheep) - At least 7 ounce (for 5 arrosticini)
- Salt

How to Prepare

Clean and wash the meat well. Do not remove the fatty pieces. Then dry it with kitchen paper.
Cut the meat into many small cubes with a maximum size of 0.6 in. (0.4 is better).
Thread the individual cubes onto the wooden skewers (wet them first for 15 minutes) until you reach halfway through the total length.
Light the BBQ in advance, with wood charcoal (do not use petroleum-based kindling materials, only odorless ones), because for cooking you will need to wait until the embers turn a gray/white color and there are no more open flames.
Place the Arrosticini on the Skewer Cooker Grill check this LINK to see what I'm talking about. https://www.agrieuro.co.uk/ferraboli-charcoal-skewer-grill-cooking-area-65x14-cm-p-29918.html)

The cooking time will be short: no more than 3 minutes per side, in case you have bought them ready-made (generally each skewer will have an average weight of 0.7 oz.) up to 5 minutes for the ones you have made yourself (average weight, 1.4. each). In any case, they should be turned as soon as they have taken on a golden color.

Serve immediately at the table and salt to taste (without exaggerating). It is essential not to allow the meat to cool.

DO NOT use any sauce or other accompaniment. Arrosticini should be eaten this way in order to fully enjoy the flavors of the Ovine meat.

Suggested Wines: In cases such as these an excellent chilled Beer is always good, or if you want to accompany them with wine, a good Montepulciano d'Abruzzo is a must.

A Variant Of Arrosticini

GRILL IT The Italian Way

Description:
This, although less traditional, is certainly a very tasty variation of the classic Arrosticini. The cooking methods are exactly the same as the previous recipe. The ingredients and the preparation of the skewers are different.

Preparation: Fast - Cooking: Fast

What's needed . per person

- Pork or Cattle Liver - 0.45 lb.
- Noble Fat of the same type – 0.22 lb.
- Onion - 1
- Fresh hot peppers (preferably Calabrian ones) - 2
- Extra Virgin Olive Oil (EVO)
- Lemon (from Sicily or the Amalfi Coast)
- Rosemary (fresh or dried)
- Salt

How to Prepare

Cut the Liver and Fat into small cube-shaped pieces (see previous recipe).
Do the same with the Onion and the Chillies.
Put on the wooden sticks (already wet for 15 minutes) alternating: 2 pieces of Fat, one of chilli, 4 of Liver and one of Onion.
Now arrange (separating them from each other) the Arrosticini on a large tray and dress them with a drizzle of EVO oil, a pinch of Rosemary and a few drops of Lemon Juice. Let stand for about 15 minutes.

Preparation and Cooking: See Previous Recipe.

Recommended Wines: See previous recipe.

The Florentine Steak

GRILL IT — The Italian Way

Description:

Here is one of the few cases where, talking about grilled meat, we Italians do not feel second to none. Of course, we are not the only ones to have excellent steaks, but the centuries-old Tuscan tradition and the breeding of some particular breeds or varieties of cattle - such as Chianina or Scottona - give us valid reasons to be proud. If you choose the right meat and the right cut and if you cook it with the right techniques... Fiorentina has nothing to envy to anyone.

Preparation: Quick - Cooking: Quick

What's needed . 2 people

- Beef (Chianina, Scottona but also, even if not Tuscan, I would not disdain a Fassona Piemontese) complete rib, that is, including the fillet and the sirloin. It must be cut thickly, so as to have a weight of "at least" 2.9 lb.
- The meat must have been aged for no less than one month.
- Coarse Salt

How to Prepare

First leave the meat out of the refrigerator for at least one hour before cooking.
The BBQ must be set up for Direct Cooking and the temperature should be set between 440 and 500 °F.
Place the steak on the grill and put some salt grains on the surface. After about 4 or 5 minutes, repeat the operation on the other side. Then, using a pair of tongs, hold the steak vertically on the grill for 1 or 2 minutes to create an even crust on the narrower sides. At the end, leave it with the Bone part directly on the Grid. The total cooking time will depend on your taste and you can judge it checking the internal temperature of the meat. It starts at 129,2 °F for rare and ends at 140 °f if you prefer it well done. Personally, I much prefer a rare cooking. Salt can also be added after cooking.
A useful trick to enhance the qualities of this recipe is to warm the dishes before serving them, so that they help to preserve the heat of the steak.
Side dishes? The "usual" barbecued potatoes, or the "usual" Pinzimonio*.

Recommended Wines: Brunello di Montalcino (Tuscany) or Barolo (Piedmont)

The Rabbit

GRILL IT — *The Italian Way*

Description:

Certainly less common than in the past, the rabbit's one is still a meat quite present in Italian eating habits, especially in small towns and in the countryside, where people still have a lifestyle more in contact with nature and less "urban". Rabbit meat is not only tasty, but being a so-called "white meat", it is also more digestible and healthy.

Preparation: Long - Cooking: Medium

What's needed. 4 people

- Breeding rabbit - from 2.9 to 4.0 lb.
- Extra Virgin Olive Oil (EVO) – 5.7 oz.
- Lemons - 1 (not chemically treated)
- Garlic - 5 or 6 cloves
- Bacon - 6 thin slices
- Rosemary (possibly fresh)
- Thyme (possibly fresh)
- Acacia Honey – 6.70 oz.
- Salt
- Black pepper to grind

How to Prepare

Wash and clean the meat well.
You can cook the Rabbit whole, but the ideal is to separate the thighs and shoulders (longer cooking time) from the rest of the body.
Prepare a marinade with the olive oil, thyme, rosemary and lemon peel finely chopped, acacia honey, lemon juice, salt and pepper.
Dip the pieces of rabbit in the marinade, soaking them evenly and then refrigerate (covered with plastic wrap) for at least a couple of hours. Obviously, at your pleasure, you can experiment with longer times, such as an entire night.

At the time of cooking, the grill must be set for direct cooking, at about 300 °F.

Start by cooking the shoulders and legs, which require a longer time. Grease the meat frequently with a sprig of rosemary, dipped in the marinade. After about 15 minutes, place on the grill the trunk of the rabbit, wrapped with the slices of bacon, blocked with toothpicks (wet). Continue to grease the meat throughout the cooking process.
In general, after another 30 minutes or so, the cooking should be completed. If necessary, check the internal temperature of the meat, which should be at least 140 °F.

Serve at table with a side dish of your choice, according to the season.

Recommended Wines: Rosso di Montefalco (Umbria) - Barbera (Piedmont)

The Boar

GRILL IT — The Italian Way

Description:

Personally I really appreciate wild boar meat, in all its forms: both as cured meats, or when it is cooked in its various ways. Particularly widespread in Umbria, Alto Lazio and Tuscany, it is precisely in Umbria that a particular memory of mine is tied to barbecuing. In the small town of Amelia in fact, there was (and there still is) a restaurant where, many years ago, an old lady prepared the best barbecued wild boar that I have ever tasted. All that remains of her now is the memory, but the wild boar is always excellent, so why miss the opportunity to cook it on the grill?

Preparation: Long - Cooking: Fast

What's needed . 4 people

- Wild Boar Meat – 2.7 lb. Preferably from young animals and as cuts, Thigh or Ribs
- Italian Red Wine* - 1.77 pt. (*see suggested wines below)
- Extra Virgin Olive Oil (EVO)
- Carrots - 2
- Garlic - 3 Cloves
- Celery stalks - 3
- Large lemons - 3
- Rosemary - better if fresh
- Salt
- Ground Black Pepper

How to Prepare

To be grilled, wild boar meat needs a thorough marinating, which must last at least 3 hours (better more). Organize yourself accordingly.
Pour the Red Wine into a suitable container and add the vegetables cut into small pieces, the Rosemary, Salt and Ground Pepper.
Now, after washing and cleaning, cut the meat into many pieces, or separate the individual ribs. Place the pieces in the marinating liquid, soaking them well. Leave in the refrigerator, covered with a sheet of aluminum. After an hour and a half, turn the meat so that it can take on flavor evenly.
Once the hours for marinating have passed, drain the boar well and keep the liquid aside. Keep at room temperature for about 60 minutes.

Set your Grill for Direct Cooking to about 340 °F, making sure there are no live flames.

Now pour a drizzle of EVO oil over the meat and then place the boar pieces on the grill. Brush it several times with the marinating liquid, perhaps using a small bunch of Rosemary. Turn the pieces halfway through cooking. Generally the total time on the grill varies between 12 and 18 minutes, depending on the thickness of the cuts you have made.

At the end of cooking, pour a little lemon juice over the boar and accompany with grilled potatoes or a pinzimonio*.

Suggested Wines: Rosso di Montefalco (Umbria) - Morellino di Scansano (Tuscany)

Larded Pheasant

GRILL IT — The Italian Way

Description:

Also this one, like wild boar, is a kind of game very used, especially in Central Italy. Currently, Pheasants are also bred and therefore it is not difficult to get their delicious meat.

Preparation: Medium - Cooking: Fast

What's needed . 4 people

- Pheasant - 1 whole
- Bacon - 1 slice for each piece of meat
- Garlic - 2 Cloves
- Onions 2
- Extra Virgin Olive Oil – 6.8 oz.
- Carrots - 2
- Salt
- Ground Black Pepper

How to Prepare

Similar to other types of game, Pheasant meat needs to be marinated beforehand. In this case, a couple hours may be enough.
Pour the oil into an appropriate container and add chopped vegetables and herbs. Also add salt and pepper to taste.

Wash and clean the pheasant well and then cut the various pieces (legs, breast, etc.) that you will dip in the marinade, wetting them well with the liquid. Turn them over every 30 minutes.

When finished, drain them well and wrap each piece of Pheasant with a slice of bacon, secured with a toothpick.

Set up the BBQ as if you were cooking Chicken in pieces (temperature between 300 and 320 °F) and place the meat on the grill for a variable time between 15 and 20 minutes, taking care to turn the pieces halfway through cooking.

Recommended Wines: Nebbiolo della Valtellina (Lombardy) - Nobile di Montepulciano (Tuscany)

Hare With Vegetables

GRILL IT — The Italian Way

Description:
Another recipe based on game. Meats that take us back to the origins of humanity, when people lived mainly on game. This time we'll talk about hare, of which we will use only the saddle.

Preparation: Quick - Cooking: Medium

What's needed. 2 people

- Hare's Saddle - 1
- Carrots - 2
- Potatoes - 2
- Apples - 2
- Onions - 1
- Extra Virgin Olive Oil (EVO)
- Salt
- Ground pepper

How to Prepare

Prepare the BBQ for Direct Cooking at 360 °F.
Wash the vegetables and dice them. Then place a cast iron Wok on the grill with some EVO oil and the finely chopped Onion. Let it brown and then add the vegetables and diced apple too. Then let them cook (with a lid) for 4 or 5 minutes. Now add about 10.15 oz. of water, Salt and Pepper to taste and let it cook for another 5 minutes. Now remove the Wok from the grill.
Place the saddle, cleaned and without its characteristic membrane, directly on the grill and brown it for about 3 minutes.
Now put the Wok back on the grill and add the Hare to the vegetables. Cover the Wok with a lid and cook for 15 - 20 minutes, until the internal temperature of the meat reaches 128 °F.

Recommended Wines: Barbera (Piedmont) or Rosso Piceno (Marche)

Apulian Lamb's Livers

GRILL IT — The Italian Way

Description:

An ancient tradition of Southern Italy and especially of Apulia, are the „Fegatelli d'Agnello". As in many Italian cases (and not only about recipes) they are called in many ways, according to the city of origin of the person who prepares them. But we don't care about names here. Their peculiarity is to be based on the entrails of the lamb: the so-called "Coratella". A mix of Lung, Liver, Heart, Spleen and so on, particularly interesting, which can appeal to different types of palates.

Preparation: Quick - Cooking: Quick

What's needed . 4 people

- Rack of lamb – 2.2 lb.
- The net and the gut of the Lamb
- Extra Virgin Olive Oil (EVO)
- Sicilian or Amalfi Coast lemons - 4
- Parsley
- Laurel (Optional)
- Salt
- Ground Black Pepper

How to Prepare

Start by washing and cleaning the entrails well. Dry them thoroughly and then pass the surfaces with Salt and the cut lemons.
Then take the various organs (Heart, Liver etc.) and cut them into strips about 0.4 – 0.5 in wide.
Mix the different strips, add pepper, finely chopped parsley and, if necessary, half of laurel leaf.
Then divide the whole, forming some roulades, 3 in. long and 1.2 in. wide at the most.
Wrap and tie each roulade with the net and the thin lamb gut.
Drizzle with a little EVO oil.

Prepare the Grill for direct cooking at a temperature of about 320 °F and clean the grill well.

Place your Livers on the grill, close the lid and let them cook for at least 30 minutes, checking them and turning them halfway through cooking.

You can accompany this dish with Tropea onions and potatoes, also made on the grill.

Recommended Wines: Primitivo di Manduria (Puglia) or Nero di Troia (Puglia)

NOTE: talking about Apulian cuisine, we suggest another cookbook from the same publisher: "Dalla Puglia con Sapore" with great and really delicious recipes. (Actually, Italian edition only) You will find the link at the end of this book.

The Bombette (Small Bombs)

GRILL IT — The Italian Way

Description:

This recipe is mainly from Martina Franca (Apulia) - one of the beautiful villages in the valley of the "Trulli" called Itria Valley. In fact, over there, a long tradition of breeding pigs and preparing cold cuts is handed down. For this recipe, in fact, the ideal is to use pork loin but, alternatively, you can also use veal slices.

Preparation: Quick - Cooking: Quick

What's needed . per person

- Thin slices of pork loin - 3
- Apulian Caciocavallo cheese (alternatively you can use the famous Caciocavallo di Agnone DOP, which comes from the neighboring region of Molise) - A small piece for each "Bombetta".
- Pancetta - 1 thin slice for each slice of meat.
- Garlic
- Fresh Parsley
- Extra Virgin Olive Oil (EVO)
- Ground Pepper
- Salt

How to Prepare

Place the slice of Bacon on one side of each slice of Meat.
Season with a mixture of Salt, Pepper, Garlic and Parsley.
Cut the Cheese into many small cubes (max 0.4 in. sideways) and place some on top of the Bacon. Be careful not to overdo it by putting too many, because you may have problems closing the wrap.
Roll up the slice and then fold the ends towards the center of the roll. Secure with wooden toothpicks. Grease each „Bombetta" well with EVO oil.

Prepare the grill for cooking meat (you know how) and place the rolls on the grill. Turn them every 3 minutes to avoid charring them. Usually 12 - 15 minutes is enough.

Serve them piping hot, with the classic Pinzimonio* of vegetables as a side dish.

Recommended Wines: Negramaro del Salento (Puglia) or Tintilia (Molise)

The Pugliese Sausage (Cervellata)

GRILL IT — The Italian Way

Description:

The classic sausage roll in the Apulian version. It has a particularity that makes it different from all the others: it is prepared by butchers according to the client's requests, with pork (in particular the leg) with veal or with a mix of the two. Often fresh wild fennel is added to the inside. So, if you are not able to get the original Pugliese one, you can always try to ask your butcher to prepare it for you.

Preparation: Quick - Cooking: Quick

What's needed . 4 people

- Pugliese Sausage (Cervellata) – 1.8 lb.
- Extra Virgin Olive Oil (EVO)
- Salt
- Ground pepper

How to Prepare

I am not going to tell you how to prepare or cook a sausage, because you will certainly know better than me, but the only peculiarity is that you must do it after cutting the „Cervellata" into pieces no longer than 4 – 4.75 in. and use EVO oil to season it before cooking. I assure you that the flavor will be amazing.

Recommended Wines: Primitivo di Manduria (Puglia) or Aglianico del Vulture (Basilicata)

Italian Sausages

GRILL IT — The Italian Way

Description:

Sausages are not exclusive to the Bel Paese, but typical Italian sausages are different from sausages, frankfurters and luganega produced in other countries. They are naturally made of pure pork, with minced meat or in very small pieces and eventually, with the addition of some aromas (for example, peppercorns or wild fennel). Some types are seasoned and then consumed raw, whereas the fresh ones can be prepared in various ways, including the BBQ. The ones from Norcia, Ariccia and generally, all the ones from Central Italy (Tuscany, Umbria, Latium) have an excellent tradition and reputation.

https://it.wikipedia.org/wiki/File:Salsiccia_Italian_pork_sausage.jpg

Preparation: Easy - Cooking: Quick

What's needed . per person

- Italian Pure Pork Sausages - 2 or 3 per person

How to Prepare

I wouldn't presume... You are the experts!
Cook them the way you like, use your preferred sauces and side dishes... the Italian „Salsicce" will always be delicious.
And beer is perfect, if you don't want to drink wine.

Recommended Wines: Chianti (Tuscany) or Rosso di Montefalco (Umbria)

Grilled Pajata

GRILL IT ◄ ──────────────────────────── **The Italian Way**

Description:

Now please: concentrate yourself in a religious silence because, as the Last Recipe, I am about to give you a secret gem (since here in Italy, the Tradition has almost been lost and only a few "Initiates" still jealously cultivate the cult) that will drive the people you'll make it taste crazy with pleasure (and envy).
There is only one adjective to describe the taste of this dish, and it's: Heavenly!
When you want to "win easy" this will be your ace in the hole!

Pajata, in Romanesco dialect (or Pagliata in Italian) is the intestine of the suckling calf (or even better of the lamb) that has never grazed the grass. I suggest you to have a good relationship with a good butcher in order to get it. The Pajata cooking (e.g. the famous Rigatoni al sugo with Pajata) is practically a Roman exclusive.

https://en.wikipedia.org/wiki/Pagliata

What's needed . 4 people

Preparation: Easy - Cooking: Quick

- Pajata of suckling calf or lamb – 1.8 lb.
- Butter – 0.45 lb.
- Ground Pepper
- Salt

How to Prepare

The first thing to do is to clean the thin lamb and delicately remove the skin without breaking it. What is contained inside must not come out. If you wonder what it is, know that it is the milk sucked by the calf or lamb.
Now cut the Pajata into many pieces about 4.5 in. long, which you can then sew at the ends with kitchen thread. Some people give them a round shape, but I prefer elongated pieces.
Separately, melt the butter and when it has melted, completely grease all the pieces.

Now place the Pajata directly on a clean grill (Direct Cooking, Temperature 310 °F) and cook it for a few minutes, turning it several times.
When it has reached a golden and crispy appearance, you can remove it from the grill, add a pinch of salt and pepper (optional) and eat it without waiting any longer.

Be careful because then you may become addicted to this true Culinary Wonder.

Recommended Wine: Red Wine of the Castelli Romani (Lazio) or Malvasia Puntinata (Lazio)

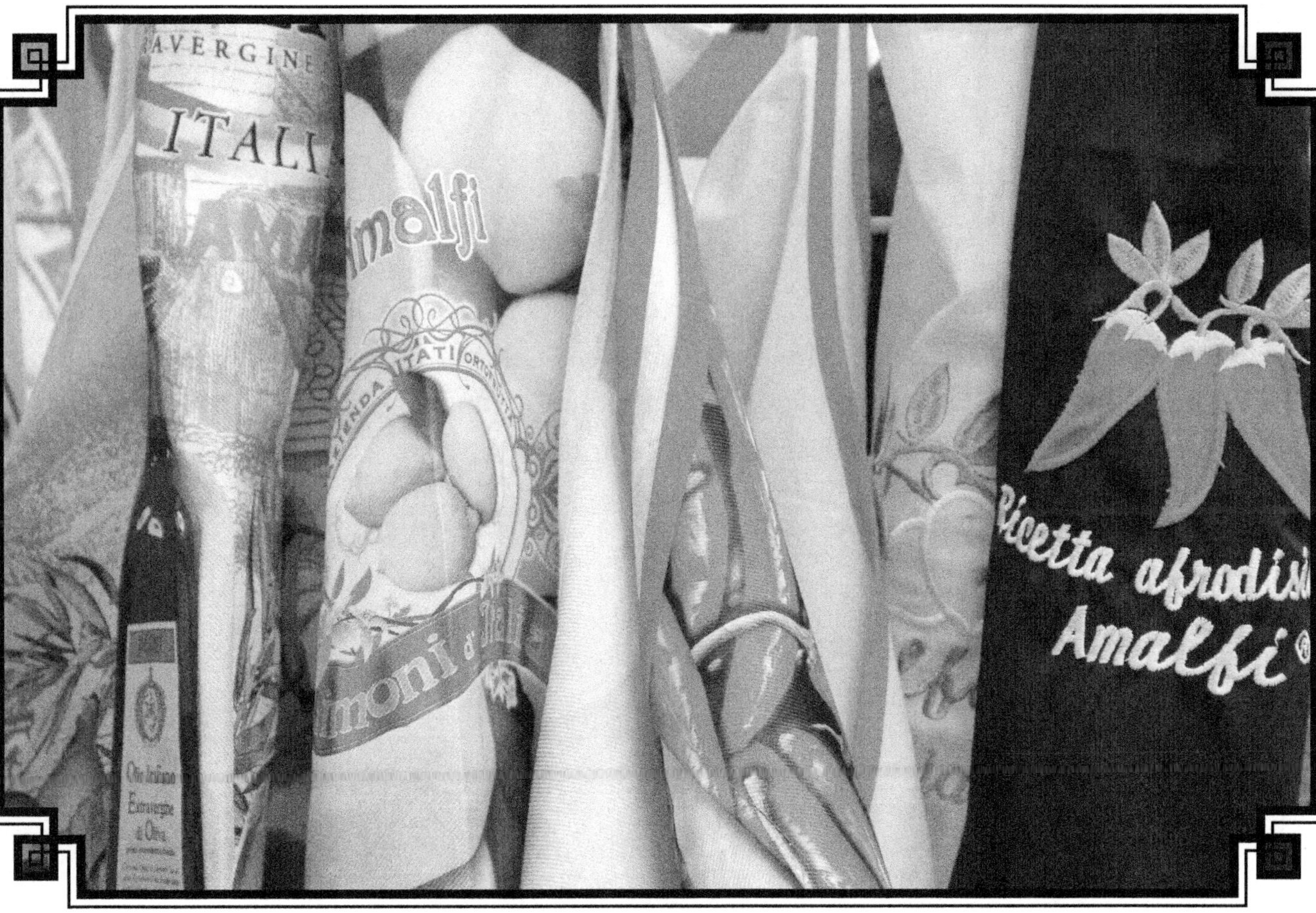
ITALI
Amalfi
Ricetta afrodisi
Amalfi

DEAR READER

To thank you for reading this book, the Publisher has come up with a BONUS for you.
You can download it for free using this QR Code

Please also take a minute of your time to review this book on Amazon. This will help other readers like you navigate when making their choices. If you were satisfied, let them know and explain why. On the other hand, if you have any criticism or want to point out some mistakes, please email us so that we can correct if possible, or otherwise always improve, the products we want to offer you.

Azad Publishing LTD
Mail: azad@azadpublishing.co.uk
Sito: https://azadpublishing.co.uk

ABOUT THE AUTHORS

Alex Amalfi

Passionate and enthusiastic connoisseur of food and wine and in particular of the traditional Italian one, he has traveled far and wide for the Bel Paese (but not only) always looking for the best recipes, products and wines that were as much as possible linked to tradition. He firmly believes that the link between cuisine and territory is the basis for a healthy and varied diet, as well as tasty and pleasant to prepare. He currently collaborates with the Editorial Group Azad Publishing Ltd. and with the web magazine iBESTmag.com

The Karing Ship Team

"Karing Ship" TEAM is the first Editorial Line of Azad Publishing Ltd. It was created to answer the fundamental question, "How to do it?" - whether it's starting a new business, learning to feel better about yourself, losing weight, gaining new skills or solving practical problems. Thanks to the experience accumulated over nearly two decades in the world of publishing and media - both traditional and online - by most of its members, our TEAM (along with selected experts, when necessary) is able to produce high quality manuals and guides to meet your needs and desires.

OTHER BOOKS FROM THE PUBLISHER

Quantum Physics for Beginners
KISS 'n Tell - A Keep It Simple Short Tale, To Understand The Secrets And The Fundamental Laws Of The Universe Through Its Compelling Story. Almost No Math Involved!
Antonio Scalisi – Karing Ship

Food Truck Business Guide For Beginners
A Step by Step Plan to Make a Living out of your Cooking Passion. Make your Dreams Come True and Be your Own Boss.
Karing Ship

Cucina Italiana - Dalla Puglia con Sapore
I Segreti di Famiglia in 50+1 Ricette Pugliesi. Dal Gargano, alla Valle d'Itria, al Salento, i Veri Sapori della … Mediterranea Pugliese. (Italian Edition)
Aurora Zito – Karing Ship

Metaverso
Tutta la Verità - La Guida Completa per Comprendere Facilmente Realtà Virtuale, Realtà Aumentata, Blockchain & Co. Come Investire con Successo su Criptovalute, NFTs e Cripto-Art. (Italian Edition)
Alan Di Marco – Karing Ship

View these books on Amazon using this QR Code

Image Credits - Images, including the Cover (modified) are from Pixabay, free commercial use. No attribution required.
pag 27 - https://it.freepik.com/foto/cibo'>Cibo foto creata da cookie_studio - it.freepik.com
pag 65 - https://it.freepik.com/foto/sfondo'>Sfondo foto creata da topntp26 - it.freepik.com
pag 27 is copyright of the Publisherwww

Printed in Great Britain
by Amazon